D0482385

Reducing Unemployment

Reducing Unemployment

A Case for Government Deregulation

Garry K. Ottosen and
Douglas N. Thompson

Westport, Connecticut
London

Library of Congress Cataloging-in-Publication Data

Ottosen, Garry K.
    Reducing unemployment : a case for government deregulation / by
Garry K. Ottosen and Douglas N. Thompson.
      p.   cm.
    Includes bibliographical references and index.
    ISBN 0-275-95360-2 (alk. paper)
    1. Full employment policies—United States. 2. Deregulation—
United States. 3. Unemployment—United States—Costs.
4. Unemployed—United States—Psychology. 5. Social problems—
United States. I. Thompson, Douglas N. II. Title.
HD5724.O78 1996
331.13'77'0973—dc20   95-30555

British Library Cataloguing in Publication Data is available.

Library of Congress Catalog Card Number: 95-30555
ISBN: 0-275-95360-2

First published in 1996

Praeger Publishers, 88 Post Road West, Westport, CT 06881
An imprint of Greenwood Publishing Group, Inc.

Printed in the United States of America

The paper used in this book complies with the
Permanent Paper Standard issued by the National
Information Standards Organization (Z39.48-1984).

10 9 8 7 6 5 4 3 2

Copyright Acknowledgment

The author and publisher gratefully acknowledge permission to quote from the following:

From *Not Working: An Oral History of the Unemployed* by Harry Maurer. Copyright © 1976
by Harry Maurer. Reprinted by permission of Henry Holt and Co., Inc.

CONTENTS

Reducing Unemployment

CHAPTER 1

THE COSTS OF UNEMPLOYMENT

S ince at least the mid-1960s, the average level of unemployment has been rising in the United States. Many policymakers seem to have accepted the increase in the so-called natural rate of unemployment without much thought as to its extremely high costs, both in terms of lost production and in human terms, and without much thought as to *why* it has been rising. Given the major unemployment problems that Europe is now experiencing, it is clear that it is past time for the United States to consider these important issues. This book focuses on the costs associated with high unemployment rates and, more important, on a systematic analysis of the fundamental causes of unemployment.

THE PERSONAL SIDE OF UNEMPLOYMENT

All too often numbers about unemployment are bandied about but the personal side of unemployment is forgotten. As unemployment is discussed in this book, let us not forget the personal side. Hence, before we begin citing numbers, let us look at a personal account of one man's unemployment experience. At the time, the late 1970s, he was 35 years old and had been fired from his job as a welder in what appears to have been an effort by the company to cut costs.[1]

> When I first applied, the unemployment office turned me down. So I had to get a lawyer, go to hearings, subpoena witnesses. It was April when I got fired, and it wasn't until the next December that the unemployment office finally decided in my favor, that I had been fired without just cause. So I didn't get any unemployment all that time. Only welfare.

It was rough. Of course, I went out almost every day at first and tried to find work, but it was in the middle of the recession. There was just no work available. There was nothing there at all. And this came as a surprise because I had never really looked for work before...

The first week I was out looking for something every day. Then slowly it got to where the money situation only allowed me to go out looking for work maybe once a week. Then it got to once every two weeks. I couldn't put gas in my car. I had like $400 worth of monthly bills. I was used to making $600 and I was cut to zero. I had money put away, enough to live on. A few dollars, not too many. It wasn't bad the first month. Well, the first two months. But after that the money depleted.

After the first thirty days it was beginning to run out. I knew in the next few weeks I was going to be at zero. So I went to welfare. Then I really had to swallow my pride. That first day at welfare was quite a day. I've tried to push it out of my mind because they really kind of step on you. I got the feeling that they have an iron hand over you, and you're nothing. I got the feeling they didn't care. They make you sit—well, it's a common thing, even in a doctor's office you hear people complaining about this. But the sitting and waiting. Waiting for nothing. And they give you as little information as they can possibly give you. I don't think—and it's a personal opinion again—I don't think they wanted to help you as much as they should have. I mean, their job is to help. I don't think they were doing their job. You get a feeling of rejection. Especially the feeling that they're better than you. No equality. No equality whatsoever. I waited all day and they told me I would have to come back the next day. I hated to go back but I knew I had to. And then they told me I couldn't draw anything for thirty days because I'd been fired. So I had to wait another month, and I didn't get my first check until July 30. From April to July, zero money.

Then there was a food stamp problem. I qualified for food stamps, but I actually had to go out on my own to find out my rights. They didn't tell me I didn't qualify for food stamps. They just didn't say anything about it....

It wasn't long before everything was gone. I had swallowed my pride and I was upset about everything. Welfare started giving us $224 a month; but they always gave you a hard time, and you had to go there almost every month for something. The fact of being off work and just laying around with no money. No money to put in the gas tank of the car to go look for work. There was the threat of the utility companies turning the electricity off. The telephone. Furnace running out of fuel all the time. They turned the phone off during that time, but I always managed to borrow some money someplace to keep the electricity from being turned off.... It got awful tough. Sometimes we'd be completely flat zero broke. We ran out of food a couple of times. No money to buy food. Wasn't nothing we could do. We just went without. We didn't eat. That's true. Sometimes for three or four days at a time.

And pretty soon you start creating your own problems. I drank a little heavy. Started drinking when there was nothing to do. When the money ran out I couldn't afford it, but any chance I got I did. And I had too much time on my hands. Too much of being home. I think it hurts your relationship, your marriage and so forth. I know in some cases of welfare the father had to leave the home to be able to survive. I wasn't gonna let that happen. I had that gnawing at me. And the wife and I had problems. We started to have little arguments. It wouldn't have happened if I'd been working. They were senseless. They were over little or nothing. We'd just bitch at each other for nothing. We had nothing else to do, just bitch at each other. I constantly raised hell because I was unhappy. She left me at one time for three or four weeks. In fact, it still affects our marriage. We see a shrink regularly. Every week. And even with going and seeing a shrink it's rough....

It's hard to even remember how I passed my time. Pushed it so far back in my mind. Even that short a time ago. You just get up in the morning and wait to go to bed at night. You can't wait till it's time to go to bed. When you go to bed you can't sleep. Worrying about things. But when you get up in the morning, you just can't wait till it's time to go to bed. You sit and wait. For what I don't know. I just kept waiting on something. That's a helluva thing to get a feeling like that. That's when it's time to see a shrink.

We had creditors after us constantly. Constantly. It got to the point where you'd look at the mail, you'd know what it was, and you just throw it aside. They just want their money, wondering when you're gonna pay. You try to explain the situation, 'cause they understand to a certain point. But they're interested in their money. They don't care about you really. I can see their point somewhat. I did keep most of my bills up, just couldn't keep them all. One month it'd be somebody, and the next it'd be somebody else. I'd revolve 'em around to where they wouldn't complain too much, but there was constantly somebody complaining. They never repossessed anything. I don't know how I did it. I really don't. Somehow I did it. There was never once a threat of repossessing.

When my wife left, that was the worst. I had a little bit of

money. Less than $100. I made that last me all month, and some-
how I managed to keep booze around pretty much of the time. I
don't know how I did it. I guess by stretching a dollar. And I had no
idea what was going to happen to me. No idea, no hopes, no nothing. Everything had went down the tubes. I knew things had to get
better because they couldn't get worse. That's the attitude I had. It's
the wrong attitude to have, I guess, but sometimes you get to a point
of wanting to give up. You know you can't give up. But when you
can't do anything, you have a feeling of total worthlessness. You're
just worthless.

As of this writing, the minimum unemployment rate attainable in the
United States consistent with stable or nonaccelerating inflation is
thought by economists to be between 6 and 7 percent of the U.S. labor
force. In other words, economists believe that to control inflation the
United States must currently keep at least 7.5 million people from working. They accept that 7.5 million people must continually go through
something like the experience of the man just recited. Why is this so? Or,
better yet, can we do anything to change the relationship between unemployment and inflation? These are the major questions we will answer in
this book.

No one will argue with the fact that forcing 7.5 million people to be
unemployed in order to control inflation is a tremendous waste. In the
coming chapters, the point is made that the relationship between unemployment and inflation can be changed. Government policies followed
during the past three decades are largely responsible for the worsening
trade-off between unemployment and inflation. These policies can and
should be changed.

HOW MUCH DOES UNEMPLOYMENT
COST THE UNITED STATES?

To begin with, let us simply state that, according to conventional economic wisdom, unemployment is the major tool available to the government to control inflation. Later in this chapter and in the next chapter, we
examine why this is believed. First, however, this introductory chapter
examines how much the use of this tool costs the United States.

In mid-1994 the United States was recovering from a recession and
had close to 9 million workers who were officially counted as unemployed, 6 million who were working part-time involuntarily and would

rather be working full-time, and at least another 1 million who had given up looking and so were not officially counted as unemployed. What does this high level of unemployment cost the United States? No generally accepted estimate of the cost of unemployment exists, but it is undoubtedly large. For instance, Graham Dawson has argued that the United States loses a little less than one percentage point of potential gross domestic product (GDP) or output for each one percentage point of unemployment.[2] This implies that an unemployment rate of 7 percent costs the United States at least $400 billion annually in forgone output. This is more than $2,000 for every man, woman, and child over 16 years of age. Even at an unemployment rate of 6 percent (the theoretical minimum to which unemployment can be reduced without kicking off inflation), the cost is still more than $340 billion or at least $1,700 per person.

Because this estimate looks only at lost output, it does not begin to add up the total cost of unemployment in the United States. In terms of social and human costs, unemployment has been linked to increases in the incidence of alcoholism, child abuse, family breakdown, vandalism and criminal behavior, psychiatric hospitalizations, suicide, homicide, and a variety of physical complaints and illnesses.[3]

Unemployment in the United States affects each and every citizen. The employed bear an economic cost, while the unemployed bear personal costs as well as economic costs. Even if we are not ourselves unemployed, we probably have a friend or family member going through the experience of the unemployed man quoted earlier. Each of us pays higher taxes and accepts a lower standard of living because millions of us are out of work. Our economy as a whole is less able to compete with other economies in the world marketplace because we carry so many unemployed persons. But while the *employed* telephone operator, grocery store manager, schoolteacher, or economist is affected by unemployment, the marginal worker bears the brunt of unemployment costs. Marginal workers are those who, because of skill level, education, physical or mental handicaps, age, race, and so, on are the first to be laid off and the last to be rehired. They are the working poor and the long-term unemployed. They spend much of their working lives dealing with unemployment, either fearing it, avoiding it, recovering from it, or fighting the reality of it. These are the people who financially and perhaps physically can least afford unemployment, yet they are the ones facing the reality of it and least able to fully recover from it.

What can be done to help these people? The answer is relatively simple: reduce the unemployment rate and put them to work in meaningful, well-paying jobs. That is what this book is about: reducing the so-called natural rate of unemployment or what some economists refer to as the nonaccelerating inflation rate of unemployment (NAIRU). At present, our economy and its workers cannot enjoy the benefits of a low-unemployment economy because every time unemployment approaches the 6-7 percent level, inflation begins to accelerate. To curb inflationary pressures, the economy is slowed by higher interest rates, allowing unemployment to rise.

WHAT WOULD BE THE BENEFITS OF LOWER UNEMPLOYMENT?

What benefits could we enjoy if the natural rate of unemployment were reduced from its present 6-7 percent range to a level of, say, 4 percent? By our earlier estimate, the first thing that would happen is that our economy would be close to $200 billion richer or nearly $800 for every man, woman, and child over age 16. More than 3.5 million more people would be employed, and the burden on our social insurance programs would be vastly reduced. Other obvious benefits would be a significant reduction in many social problems that have been exacerbated by high unemployment—problems such as alcoholism, child abuse, family breakdown, criminal behavior, psychiatric hospitalization, suicide, and so on. Somewhat less obviously, all U.S. workers would benefit from the competition by employers for employees.

In a low-unemployment economy, or tight labor market, employers are forced to compete with one another to hire and hold employees. This competition must take the form of offering good pay and benefit packages and a good working environment. A cursory look at federal and state government laws and regulations shows a belief on the part of government officials that workers need to be protected from employers and that employers must be forced through legislation to provide good working environments. Competition for employees would accomplish the same thing without the huge costs associated with a government-imposed bureaucracy and legal apparatus. If the unemployment rate were low enough or, conversely, if employment opportunities plentiful enough, employers would offer their employees family leave, flexible work schedules, and clean, comfortable environments free of discrimination and harassment. Desiring to hire and hold quality workers and not face the costs of high turnover and low employee morale, employers would willingly provide better conditions for all employees.

CAN WE TRADE HIGHER INFLATION FOR LOWER UNEMPLOYMENT?

The costs of using high unemployment to control inflation are simply too high, and the benefits of a low-unemployment society are simply too great for us to continue without making a serious effort to reduce the level of unemployment consistent with stable inflation. Given this truth, several questions come immediately to mind. First, if the costs of high unemployment are so high, and the benefits of low unemployment so great, why don't we simply push down the unemployment rate and forget about inflation? We cannot do this for several reasons.

The first reason is that doing so is simply too expensive in terms of damage to the economy. A market economy depends critically on prices carrying accurate information about relative abundance and scarcity, about supply and demand. Inflation, especially inflation of the accelerating, unstable sort, introduces a great deal of uncertainty into the economy. Just as an architect has a difficult time building sound structures using unstable supports, so we cannot build a sound economy using unstable, unpredictable prices. Eventually, if inflation is allowed to continue to accelerate, any market economy will collapse.

If the rate of inflation were perfectly predictable, most of inflation's ill effects could be avoided. Contracts, wages, interest rates, and the tax system could take future inflation into account, and it would make little difference to economic performance whether the rate was 0 percent or 5 percent. Because inflation is not predictable, it damages economies.

Unforeseen inflation stunts growth because it distorts the price mechanism, by making it difficult to distinguish changes in relative prices from changes in the general price level. If apples are rising in price relative to other fruit, this ought to attract new apple growers and encourage consumers to buy some other fruit instead. But general inflation obscures the relative movement; neither fruit buyers nor fruit growers take much note of a 20 percent jump in apple prices when other fruits have gone up 15 percent. So resources are misallocated, and growth is consequently slower than it could have been. Even with a relatively low annual inflation rate of 5 percent, prices double every 14 years, swamping most relative price changes. If the general price level is stable, the market economy functions better.

A second effect of inflation is uncertainty, and uncertainty is the enemy of investment and growth. If businesspeople are unsure of the future level of prices and hence of real interest rates, they will be less willing to take risks and to invest, especially in long-term projects. Inflation encourages a preoccupation with short-term profits at the expense of longer-term returns. Furthermore, uncertainty about inflation pushes up real interest rates, as lenders demand a bigger risk premium on their money. High real interest rates stifle economic growth.

In years past, the now-famous Phillips curve led many to believe that we could trade higher inflation for lower unemployment. But the trade-off implied by the Phillips curve has proven to be unstable in the short term and nonexistent in the long term. In other words, we might be able to reduce unemployment in the short term by accepting higher inflation, but in the long term we will simply end up with higher inflation and, at best, no improvement in unemployment. In the 1970s, we ended up with the worst possible scenario: higher inflation plus higher unemployment. The next chapter discusses the Phillips curve in more detail.

Another reason we cannot hope to trade higher inflation for lower unemployment is that today's financial markets will simply not allow it to happen. Having gone through the inflationary period from the late 1960s through the 1970s consistently underestimating the severity and longevity of inflation and getting burned because of it, financial market participants are not about to ignore inflationary signals again. If any government were to try to push down the unemployment rate and forget about inflation, financial market participants would quickly push up interest rates enough to protect themselves against inflation with a significant risk premium tacked on top. The higher interest rates would act like a brake on the economy, slowing it and preventing the unemployment rate from falling.

To summarize, the cost of high unemployment is extremely large and the benefit of low unemployment is great, but we cannot minimize the cost and maximize the benefits by artificially pushing the unemployment rate below the level consistent with stable inflation. It simply costs too much and won't work anyway.

HOW DO WE LOWER THE NATURAL UNEMPLOYMENT RATE?

What, then, can we do? The answer is simple enough: make unemployment more effective at controlling inflation so that less of it will be needed; in other words, reduce the "natural" level of unemployment needed to control inflation. But isn't the natural rate of unemployment just that—natural? It most certainly is not. It is a function of many factors that can be changed. Given the terrible costs of unemployment, it is our responsibility to at least ask if we can change the fundamental factors in our economy that affect the natural rate of unemployment.

The experience of low-unemployment economies like that of Sweden offers hope. Until quite recently, Sweden's natural rate of unemployment was less than 3 percent. In other words, at most, only 3 percent of Sweden's workers needed to be unemployed to keep inflation under control. Obviously, Sweden's unemployment was more effective at controlling inflation than was the United States' unemployment.

Furthermore, the United States' natural rate of unemployment has not always been as high as 6 to 7 percent. In the 1960s, it was around 4 to 5 percent. Given the fact that Swedish unemployment has been very effective at controlling inflation and that U.S. unemployment was once much more effective than it is now, we must conclude that we can do more than we are currently doing to make sure that we have the barest minimum number of unemployed people consistent with stable inflation.

We most certainly do not want to continue the trend of the past two decades toward an ever-increasing natural unemployment rate. Great Britain once had a natural rate of unemployment below 4 percent. It now has a natural rate of unemployment of 8 percent. In other words, even in prosperous times its unemployment rate cannot drop below 8 percent. This represents a huge waste of talent, skills, and resources. It represents millions of personal tragedies. Great Britain cannot long afford this. The United States cannot afford its 6-7 percent natural unemployment rate, let alone following Great Britain to the 8 percent or higher level.

How, then, do we do it? How do we make our unemployment more effective and thus reduce our unemployment rate without allowing inflation to accelerate? The simple and quite correct answer is that we must get better at controlling inflation without having to resort to increasing unemployment. The government needs more tools to use in controlling inflation.

Implicit in the foregoing discussion is the assumption that the only way the government can effectively control inflation is to restrict demand by using monetary or fiscal policy to slow the economy, reduce capacity utilization, and force the unemployment rate up. But restricting demand is not the only tool the government can use. It can pursue policies that promote productivity growth; it can fight structural or mismatch unemployment; it can reduce the disincentives to work that many of our social programs contain; and it can vigorously pursue cost containment in its regulatory functions. These and other policies that are discussed in this book can reduce the amount of unemployment needed to control inflation.

The benefits of a low-unemployment economy will flow not just to previously unemployed workers but to all workers. Current thinking on unemployment focuses on the benefits that may flow to unemployed workers who are removed from the unemployment rolls through retraining or other programs. This approach implicitly accepts a natural unemployment rate of 6–7 percent. Achieving a low-unemployment economy, a tight labor market, will benefit, first and foremost, the marginal workers who will get and hold on to decent jobs. But the benefits do not stop there. All workers will benefit as a low-unemployment economy increases competitive pressures on employers to hire and hold on to good employees.

NOTES

1. From Harry Maurer, *Not Working: An Oral History of the Unemployed* (New York: Holt, Rinehart & Winston, 1979). Reprinted by permission of Henry Holt and Co., Inc.

2. Graham Dawson, *Inflation and Unemployment: Causes, Consequences and Cures* (Brookfield, VA: Edward Elgar, 1992), Chapter 7; the International Monetary Fund (IMF) has also pointed out that "the long-run economic cost, measured as a percent of GDP, is of the same order of magnitude as the unemployment rate itself," in *World Economic Outlook* (Washington, DC: IMF, May 1994), p. 35.

3. Nick Kates, Barres S. Greiff, and Duane Q. Hagen, *The Psychological Impact of Job Loss* (Washington, DC: American Psychiatric Press, 1990), p. 38.

CHAPTER 2

THE NAIRU

In Chapter 1, the concept of a natural rate of unemployment was briefly mentioned. As discussed, this is the rate of unemployment below which the economy cannot be pushed and still expect to have stable inflation. This rate is perhaps more accurately called the nonaccelerating inflation rate of unemployment or NAIRU. In other words, it is the unemployment rate that is consistent with stable or nonaccelerating inflation. Economists disagree over whether the two terms refer to the same thing, but this book will not debate that issue. For our purposes, *the NAIRU* and *the natural rate of unemployment* both refer to that rate of unemployment that is consistent with stable or nonaccelerating inflation. Given this definition, *NAIRU* is the more accurate term and is the term used in our examination of unemployment levels and inflation.

What is the NAIRU, and why does it exist? What determines it, and what causes it to change? How do government policies affect the NAIRU, and can government policies reduce it? These are the questions addressed in this chapter.

THE EXISTENCE OF A NAIRU

Let us begin by providing some evidence that a NAIRU does exist in the United States and discussing why it exists. To document more clearly the existence of a NAIRU in the United States, evidence of an unemployment rate below which inflation begins to accelerate or an unemployment rate that is consistent with stable inflation is presented.

The Evidence

One of the best-known economists to work in the area of identifying the U.S. NAIRU is Robert J. Gordon. To estimate the NAIRU, or natural rate as he calls it, Gordon uses a statistical equation relating inflation to aggregate unemployment. A NAIRU series is then generated by solving for that unemployment rate at which inflation is unchanging. Figure 2.1 shows Gordon's estimated NAIRU time series from 1953 to 1985.[1]

One of the most recent estimates of the NAIRU comes from Stuart E. Weiner. He uses a methodology similar to that used by Robert Gordon, but he adjusts his estimates for demographic and structural changes. His estimates, covering the period from 1961 to 1992, are also included in Figure 2.1.[2] In addition, the figure also shows other estimates of the NAIRU, provided by Weiner in an earlier paper, that form an upper and lower band.[3] The estimates of the NAIRU included in this figure illustrate the fact that the exact level of the NAIRU in the United States is difficult to determine, but the fact of its existence is challenged by very few. Any economist's estimate of the NAIRU depends on the assumptions, specific model, and data employed. Still, the time series shown in Figure 2.1 with its upper and lower bands is likely to contain the actual NAIRU for the United States.

One thing that should be obvious from these estimates of the U.S. NAIRU is that it has been rising. In 1953, the NAIRU was estimated to be between 3.5 and 5 percent; by 1990, it was between 6 and 7 percent. In general, most economists who study the NAIRU would agree with the statement that it rose from about 5 percent in the 1960s to just above 7 percent in the 1970s and then declined to about 6.5 percent in the 1980s.[4]

Recently, Richard Vedder and Lowell Gallaway have attempted to estimate the U.S. NAIRU using a 10-year weighted average of unemployment.[5] Figure 2.2 shows such a weighted average together with Weiner's estimate of the NAIRU for comparative purposes. Without going into details of Vedder and Gallaway's argument, let us examine why such a weighted average of unemployment rates might approximate the NAIRU. A 10-year weighted average incorporates the yearly unemployment rates during at least two business cycles and is therefore a good approximation of the long-term unemployment rate. A justification for using the *long-term* unemployment rate as an estimate of the NAIRU is that, in the long run, the unemployment rate is likely, at times, to bounce below the NAIRU and trigger inflation; it is also likely to be pushed above the NAIRU to combat inflation at other times; the unemployment rate's long-

FIGURE 2.1
HIGH AND LOW NAIRU ESTIMATES VERSUS
10-YEAR WEIGHTED AVERAGE*

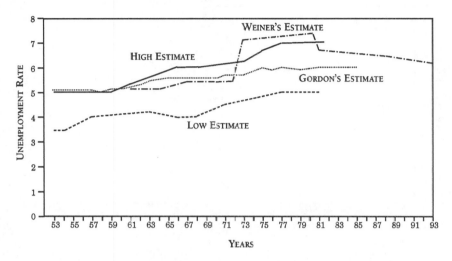

* Sources: Robert J. Gordon, *Marcoeconomics*, 4th ed. (Boston: Little, Brown, 1987), Appendix A; Stuart E. Weiner, "New Estimates of the Natural Rate of Unemployment," *Federal Reserve Bank of Kansas City Economic Review* 78 (Fourth Quarter 1993), pp. 53-69; and Stuart E. Weiner, "The Natural Rate of Unemployment: Concepts and Issues," *Federal Reserve Bank of Kansas City Economic Review* 71 (January 1986), pp. 11-24.

run average may very well approximate the NAIRU.

A comparison of the 10-year weighted average and estimates by Robert Gordon and Stuart Weiner of the natural rate of unemployment lends some support to the view that the long-run unemployment rate is an appropriate estimate of the NAIRU. All of the estimates of the NAIRU show an overall increase between the early 1950s and the late 1970s. Gordon estimates an increase from about 5 percent to about 6 percent. Weiner estimates an increase from about 5 percent to about 7 percent. The 10-year moving-average estimate increased from about 4 percent to about 7 percent. Differences between the estimates obviously exist, but the main point is that they show that the unemployment rate that is compatible with stable or nonaccelerating inflation increased significantly between the 1950s and the 1980s. Virtually all economists who have analyzed the NAIRU (or whatever they may call it) have reached a similar conclusion.[6]

FIGURE 2.2
ESTIMATES OF THE U.S. NAIRU*

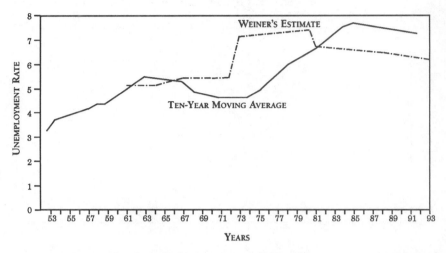

* Sources: Richard K. Vedder and Lowell E. Gallaway, *Out of Work* (New York: Holmes and Meier, 1993), and Stuart E. Weiner, "New Estimates of the Natural Rate of Unemployment," *Federal Reserve Bank of Kansas City Economic Review* 78 (Fourth Quarter 1993), pp. 53-69.

Some economists now argue that the NAIRU declined significantly in the early 1990s. Robert Gordon, for instance, has argued that productivity gains and the weakness of labor unions have made possible a decline in the NAIRU from about 6 percent to about 5.5 percent. Even one of the originators of the NAIRU concept, Edmund Phelps, has argued that it may have declined from about 6.5 percent to about 6 percent. He cites changes in public assistance programs as contributing to this decline.[7]

The Phillips Curve

At this point, a very brief discussion of the so-called Phillips curve is perhaps helpful. In 1958, Bill Phillips, a New Zealand economist, published a paper entitled "The Relation between Unemployment and the Rate of Change of Money Wages in the United Kingdom, 1861-1957."[8] In this paper, Phillips documented a stable trade-off between inflation and unemployment—the more you had of the one, the less you had of the other. Figure 2.3 plots inflation (looking directly at prices, not at wages) and unemployment in the United States during the 1960s. The points fall on a fairly neat, downward-sloping line—the so-called Phillips curve. The

FIGURE 2.3
THE U.S. PHILLIPS CURVE DURING THE 1960s:
INFLATION VERSUS UNEMPLOYMENT*

PHILLIPS CURVE 1960–69

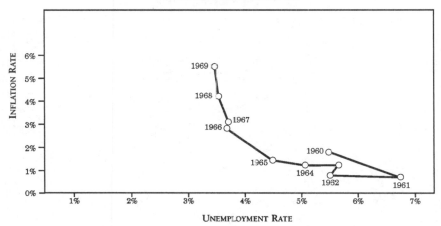

*Source: Department of Labor, Bureau of Labor Statistics, *Employment and Earnings*, various issues.

United States during the 1960s appeared to have a stable Phillips curve, with the implication that the government could cut unemployment by tolerating a higher rate of inflation.

Until the end of the 1960s, most economists accepted the concept of a stable relationship between unemployment and inflation—a stable Phillips curve. But that acceptance changed in the 1970s as the Phillips curve faced two separate but effective attacks, one from economic theory and the other from the real world.

The theoretical attack was led by Milton Friedman and Edmund Phelps, who, in separate papers, asserted that the theory underlying the curve made no sense.[9] Both economists pointed out that while the Phillips curve was based on nominal or money wages, in reality, real (or inflation-adjusted) wages matter to both workers and employers. For example, suppose that wage and price inflation increases by five percentage points from, say, 3 percent annually to 8 percent annually. Under the Phillips curve type of analysis, based on nominal wages and/or prices, we would expect unemployment to go down. But, in reality, real wages have not changed. The demand for labor and the supply of labor, both of

FIGURE 2.4
THE U.S. PHILLIPS CURVE DURING 1970-93:
INFLATION VERSUS UNEMPLOYMENT*

PHILLIPS CURVE 1970-93

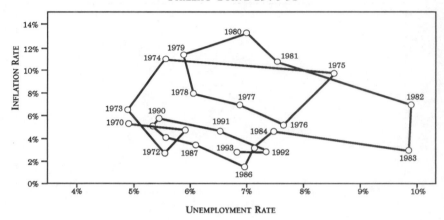

*Source: Department of Labor, Bureau of Labor Statistics, *Employment and Earnings*, various issues.

which depend on real wages, have also not changed. That being the case, we cannot expect the employment situation to change. The Phillips curve cannot be right.

The only complication arises if workers suffer from so-called money illusion. Suppose prices rise unexpectedly, and because workers are slow to recognize that inflation has accelerated, wages do not quickly follow. Further suppose that workers, whose expectations about inflation are inaccurate, are slow to realize that their wages have fallen in real terms. In this situation, the workers will not reduce their supply of labor, but employers will increase their demand for labor. This increase in the demand for labor will cause employment to expand. In this way, an unexpected rise in inflation may cut unemployment.

What happens, however, when workers' expectations catch up to reality? Suppose that inflation holds steady at its new, higher rate. Workers realize that their wages have fallen in real terms. They bid for higher pay to catch up, and as they succeed, and real wages return to their previous level, the demand for labor falls back, and unemployment rises to its previous level. Once money illusion has dissipated, the employment level and real wages are as before. Only the rate of inflation is different: it is permanently higher.

The theoretical attack on the Phillips curve was not yet fully acknowledged when experience in the real world began to undermine faith in the Phillips curve. Figure 2.4 shows the relationship between inflation and unemployment during the period from 1970 to 1993. The relationship, obviously, is no longer a nice, neat curve. Inflation and unemployment are no longer linked in such a way as to suggest an exploitable trade-off.

Today, economists no longer talk about a Phillips curve. Rather, they identify two Phillips curves: a short-run Phillips curve and a long-run Phillips curve. Figure 2.5 shows both a short-run and a long-run Phillips curve. Let us suppose that the economy starts at a point such as A, with unemployment of U1 and an inflation rate of P1. Next suppose that the government pushes up the inflation rate to P2. In the short run, unemployment falls to U2; the economy moves to point B on the short-run Phillips curve. Gradually, however, expectations adjust, the economy moves back toward equilibrium, and unemployment starts to rise again. The economy moves to point C, on the longer-run Phillips curve. Inflation is still P2, but now unemployment has risen to U3. When expectations have adjusted fully, the long-run Phillips curve is actually vertical. With inflation still at P2, the economy has moved to point D. Unemployment has returned to U1, leaving the economy unambiguously worse off: as many people are out of work as before, and the inflation rate is higher.

FIGURE 2.5

THE SHORT-RUN, LONGER-RUN, AND LONG-RUN PHILLIPS CURVES

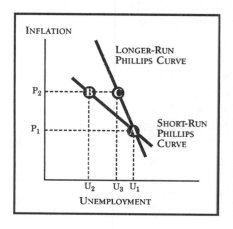
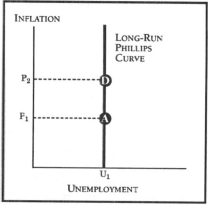

Theory and experience teach us that there is no permanent trade-off between inflation and unemployment. In the long run, regardless of the inflation rate, the economy returns to its underlying rate of unemployment. This underlying rate is the nonaccelerating inflation rate of unemployment, the NAIRU.

Why Does the NAIRU Exist?

The term "*NAIRU*" implies that a link between the unemployment rate and the inflation rate exists. We must understand why such a linkage exists before we can understand what causes the NAIRU to increase and decrease and before we can determine what policies can be used to reduce it.

Why does such a thing as a NAIRU exist? Why does inflation start to accelerate if the unemployment rate is pushed below a certain point? Economists have long pointed out that in trying to understand why the NAIRU exists, it is useful to distinguish among three distinct types of unemployment.[10]

First, there is *frictional unemployment*. Frictional unemployment arises as a result of the normal labor turnover that occurs in a healthy dynamic economy. At any given time employed workers change jobs, lose jobs, or leave the labor force. Similarly, unemployed workers may find employment or may decide to stop seeking employment, while still others may enter or reenter the labor force. Even in the best of times some unemployment arises from this dynamic friction in the economy.

The type of unemployment that is perhaps perceived and felt most acutely is *cyclical unemployment*. As its name suggests, it is the type of unemployment that is associated with business cycles. Decreases in aggregate demand that occur during recessions cause a general overall decline in labor demand. Workers are laid off, and cyclical unemployment results.

The third type of unemployment is probably the least understood and perhaps the most traumatic to endure. Unlike cyclical unemployment, *structural unemployment* is the result of shifts in the relative demand for different types of labor. These relative shifts in labor demand may be caused by changes in relative factor prices (e.g., an oil price shock), technological innovations, changes in tastes and preferences, or changes in institutional or other characteristics of the economy.

Structural unemployment can also be the result of demographic change. For instance, inexperienced youth may increase as a percentage of the labor force as a baby boom generation enters the working years.

Employers may not be able to train and employ all of the youth desiring work, and increased unemployment may result as the economy adjusts to the changing demographic situation.

Structural unemployment can also result from a geographic mismatch, where workers are located in one area and employers in another, and mobility between the areas is, for some reason, restricted.

Sometimes analysts include only unemployment due to demographic factors, regional mismatch, and skill mismatch in their definition of structural unemployment. But as defined here, structural unemployment includes unemployment that results from trade shocks, changes in social welfare transfers, and any factor that is not frictional or cyclical in nature. We refer to unemployment that results from demographic changes, regional mismatch, or skill mismatch as simply mismatch unemployment, to make clear the point that structural unemployment can result from more than just these three factors.

Theoretically, structural unemployment is only temporary because, in time, those who are structurally unemployed will either retrain to find employment in the now higher labor demand industries, relocate to find jobs requiring the types of skills they already have, or perhaps leave the labor force altogether, in which case they are not counted as unemployed. How long this process takes depends on the costs of education, the costs associated with relocating or finding employment farther from one's original location, the costs of job search, and additional opportunity and psychological costs.

In terms of these three components, the NAIRU is simply the rate that would occur in the absence of cyclical fluctuations. It is the sum of frictional and structural unemployment.

Robert Gordon provides a useful example utilizing the concepts of frictional and structural unemployment to explain why a NAIRU exists. Suppose there exists an economy in which the NAIRU is zero. All of the jobs in this economy are completely identical in their skill requirements, and all are located at exactly the same place. All workers are completely identical, with their skills perfectly suited for the identical jobs; furthermore, all workers live in the same location as the jobs. Gordon asks us to imagine a 10-mile-high combined factory-office-apartment skyscraper with very fast elevators.

Gordon points out that vacancies and unemployment cannot simultaneously exist in this imaginary economy. Suppose that initially some workers are cyclically unemployed and that the government pursues expansive monetary and/or fiscal policies to stimulate demand.

Additional jobs open up, but the unemployed workers are in exactly the right place and possess the right skills. They instantly zoom to the jobs' locations on the speedy elevators, the job vacancies disappear immediately, and unemployment declines.

If the stimulus to aggregate demand continues, eventually all of the unemployed will find jobs. Any job vacancies that exist after all the cyclically unemployed workers have found jobs will remain unfilled. More aggregate demand stimulus will just expand the number of job vacancies.

Gordon asks us to change this scenario slightly and assume there are now two types of jobs and two types of workers in our imaginary economy, typists and computer programmers. As the economy expands, it gradually uses up its supply of trained computer programmers. Once all of them have jobs, all of the unemployment consists of jobless typists. If the government further stimulates aggregate demand, we assume that an equal number of job vacancies is created for programmers and typists. The typist vacancies disappear immediately as available typists are carried by the elevators to fill the job openings. But there are no computer programmers left, and so the programmer job openings remain. Vacancies and unemployment exist simultaneously because firms refuse to hire typists to fill programmer vacancies. The costs of training are just too high. If training were costless, typists could fill the programmer vacancies, and there would be no remaining vacancies or unemployment.

In reality, our economy is divided into numerous separate labor markets differing in location, working conditions, and skill requirements. In our imaginary economy with all jobs and workers alike and located at the same place, policymakers could use aggregate demand stimulus to push the unemployment rate to zero. But in the real-world economy, with its numerous separate labor markets, vacancies and unemployment can and do coexist. Any attempt to use aggregate demand policy to push the total unemployment rate to zero will create numerous job vacancies for the types of skills that are in short supply and in the locations where labor is scarce. Firms desperate to hire workers will boost wage rates hoping to steal workers from other firms. Higher wages will raise business costs and cause price increases. Thus, according to Gordon, a situation with a low unemployment rate and lots of job vacancies maintained through demand growth is one in which the inflation rate will continuously accelerate.

How low can policymakers push the unemployment rate without causing inflation to accelerate? This depends, according to Gordon, on how much upward pressure on wages is created by each job vacancy, compared to downward pressure on wages created by each unemployed worker. This, in essence, is what determines the natural rate of unemployment or NAIRU.

To understand the NAIRU better we must understand the relationship between real wages and unemployment. This will lead us to an examination of the determinants of the NAIRU.

WHAT DETERMINES THE NAIRU

The theory of how real wages relate to unemployment is very simple. In a nutshell, there is, at any particular time, a limit to the living standard that the economy can provide to its workers. This is determined by productivity. In other words, there is a "feasible real wage." If workers and/or their bargaining agents succeed in increasing nominal wages faster than this, inflation will increase—with wages accelerating and prices following. Stable inflation requires that workers do not demand wage increases that are, on average, higher than the economy's rate of feasible real wage growth. The unemployment rate plays a crucial role in letting wage bargainers know when their desired or target real wage is out of line with the economy's feasible real wage. As Richard Layard has pointed out, just enough unemployment will ensure that the "target" real wage equals the "feasible" real wage. If there is "not enough" unemployment, nominal wages will be pushed too high, and wage inflation will increase. Alternatively, if there is "excess" unemployment, wage and price inflation will fall.[11]

In summary, if workers try to get real wages that are too high relative to feasible real wages, inflation will spiral upward. What eventually stops this? The answer is that the wage bargainers eventually adjust their behavior, for their behavior depends, to an extent, on unemployment. If inflation is increasing, governments will allow unemployment to increase. This will dampen wage pressure. Thus, higher unemployment will reduce the target real wage until it is equal to what is feasible. The NAIRU is the level of unemployment at which there is just enough unemployment to make wage bargainers settle on the real wage that firms are capable of delivering.

What happens if the government stimulates demand and creates so many jobs that unemployment falls below the NAIRU? In this situation wage bargainers push wage inflation above expected price inflation (more, that is, than any difference due to productivity growth). Because they underestimate the rise of price inflation induced by their actions, they do not hit the real wage at which they were aiming, but they do get some increase in real wages. Firms provide this increase because they, too, underestimated the rise in wages and so allowed their price markup over actual wages to fall. So rising inflation was the device that reconciled the behavior of wage bargainers and the marketing managers of firms.[12]

Using the framework of a feasible real wage and a target real wage just presented, we can analyze the events that might increase an economy's NAIRU. The NAIRU will be stable if increases in the feasible real wage are in line with increases in the target real wage. But complications with this reasoning can come from two sources. First, something can cause changes in the feasible real wage to drop below what might otherwise be expected. Second, wage setters might push increases in the target real wage beyond increases in the feasible real wage. Either event will lead to an increase in the NAIRU.[13]

An examination of factors that may cause increases in the feasible or potential real wage to drop below expectations follows.

Business Costs

Any event, other than increases in labor costs, that increases business costs will cause prices to rise at any given level of money wages. In other words, real wages will fall, and the feasible real wage will fall. One of the most often discussed events that increased business costs is the Organization of Petroleum Exporting Countries (OPEC)-induced oil price increase in 1973-74. This is an example of a trade shock. Other events that might cause business costs to increase include food price increases due to droughts, floods, and so on; increases in the prices of industrial commodities other than oil, like gold, silver, steel, or lumber, due to supply conditions; and increases in government regulations that impose costs on businesses. These events can cause costs to businesses to increase without increasing the economy's productive capacity. The prices of finished goods must therefore rise, and the feasible real wage level in the economy must decline. As this feasible real wage declines, and the target real wage does not, the NAIRU increases.

Looking at this from a slightly different point of view, any event that causes costs to business to rise without increasing productivity will increase prices to consumers. In other words, the Consumer Price Index will rise, and with it, inflation. As inflation rises, the federal government will be forced to increase unemployment to control it. The level of unemployment consistent with stable inflation will therefore increase with any event that increases business costs without increasing productivity.

Productivity Growth Rate

The feasible or potential real wage that any economy can support depends critically on the rate of growth of productivity. A man cannot run faster than his legs will carry him, and real wages cannot long increase faster than the growth rate of output per worker. If the rate of productivity growth falls, and wage setters do not adjust their target real wage accordingly, then inflation will increase, and unemployment will rise to make wage setters accept the new reality. Therefore, any factor that reduces productivity growth has the potential to increase the NAIRU, depending critically on whether wage setters recognize and accept a slow-down in real wage growth. Similarly, any factor that increases productivity growth has the potential to reduce the NAIRU. This is an important point to keep in mind in discussing things that can be done to reduce the NAIRU.

Taxes

Another force that could reduce feasible real wages is tax increases. Tax increases obviously reduce real take-home pay but may not reduce the real wages sought by workers. If workers do not reduce their desired real wage in the face of a tax increase, then the NAIRU will increase.

Increases in business costs, slowdowns in productivity growth, and increases in taxes all have the potential to increase the NAIRU by lowering the feasible real wage. Factors that may increase the NAIRU by increasing workers' target or desired real wage follow.

Social Welfare Benefits and Policies

One factor that obviously increases the target real wage of workers is unemployment insurance or benefits. If workers who become unemployed have a continuing income, they obviously will be reluctant to take the first job that comes along. In fact, depending on how generous their unemployment benefits are, they may actually be better off remaining idle rather than taking a low-wage job. Surely, target real wages increase with increases in unemployment benefits. Therefore, the more generous the benefits, the higher the NAIRU.

A similar argument can be made for minimum wage laws. Such laws increase the target real wage of workers and therefore increase the NAIRU.

Minimum wage laws have a pronounced effect on teenage unemployment. Some employers simply will not hire teenagers because the minimum wage is too high. This is doubly bad for our economy because we lose not only output from forgone production but also the future benefit that would come from teenagers who have developed a strong work ethic.

Unemployment benefits are not the only benefits that increase the target real wage of workers. In general, all welfare benefits that allow able-bodied individuals to forgo work increase the NAIRU. This is not to say that the safety net has no value or place in our society, but let us recognize its costs, both direct and indirect. In formulating social policies, governments must keep in mind the work incentives or disincentives of each policy.

At this point, mention should be made of long-term unemployment. We have pointed out that high unemployment exerts a downward pressure on inflation mainly by restraining wages. Any factor that makes wages more sensitive to unemployment will make unemployment better at its job and will reduce the NAIRU. The opposite is also true. Any factor that makes wages less sensitive to unemployment increases the NAIRU. Long-term unemployment reduces the sensitivity of wages to unemployment because the long-term unemployed have nearly dropped out of the labor force and do not vigorously compete for jobs. Therefore, any policy that increases the percentage of all unemployed persons who are long-term unemployed will increase the NAIRU. If unemployment or welfare benefits are extended, and long-term unemployment increases as a result, then the NAIRU will increase as well.

Mismatch

Another factor that may increase the economy's target real wage is mismatch. Mismatch was already mentioned in our discussion of structural unemployment. Suffice it here to say that any factor or policy that increases the mismatch between job skills required and job skills available in any location will increase the NAIRU. As already mentioned, factors that may increase mismatch unemployment are divided into three general categories: demographic factors, regional factors, and skill factors.

Demographic factors obviously include changes in the composition of the labor force that worsen the match between skills required and skills available. Regional factors include anything that worsens the locational dimensions of mismatch, such as a mass movement of firms from the so-called Rust Belt to the so-called Sun Belt. Factors or policies that decrease workers' mobility also increase mismatch. If a change in the economy occurs such that Alaska needs the skilled craftspersons who live in Alabama, but those skilled craftspersons have no incentive to move, then the NAIRU will increase. If those skilled craftspersons are actually willing to move, even hungry for the opportunity to use their skills, but never find out about the jobs in Alaska, then the effect on NAIRU is the same as if the craftspersons were unwilling to move or did not even exist. Poor information flows can also increase the NAIRU.

Finally, skill factors include anything that may cause the level of skills required to diverge from the level of skills available. An example of a skill factor is a shift in the economy from one based on low-tech industries to one based on high-tech industries that is not accompanied by improved education of workers. In this regard, a primary and secondary education system that does not provide quality workers is a factor that can worsen structural mismatch. Poor postsecondary educational opportunities such as limited access to technical training and schools, limited apprenticeship programs, and overly expensive or restrictive community college and university systems also contribute to the mismatch problem and thus increase the NAIRU.

Union Power

Union pressure on wage rates is also a factor that can increase the target real wage and thus increase the NAIRU. Any policy that gives labor unions more power to achieve high relative wages might worsen the trade-off between inflation and unemployment. We say might, not will, because union leaders must be conscious not only of their members' wage levels but also of the impact those wage levels have on their members' employment and unemployment. For instance, unions in Sweden are economy-wide in nature. Some analysts argue that because of this they must look at the big picture when bargaining with employers over wage levels. Union leaders know that if they push wages too high, employment will suffer. They may value full employment in the economy as much as high wages and may therefore restrain their wage demands.

This is not the case for unions in most countries, including the United States. We can reasonably argue that in the United States the relationship between high wage increases and unemployment is at best fuzzy in the minds of most union leaders. Their major goal is to push wages and benefits as high as possible. They rely primarily on counterpressure from management to determine how high is too high and only secondarily on the level of unemployment.

Let us examine briefly one way that excessively high relative wages, whether union or nonunion, can cause the NAIRU to increase. If workers in a particular firm manage to collect wages that are high compared to similar workers using similar levels of capital equipment in other firms, then the mangers of the high-wage firm will at least find it advantageous to lay off some workers and increase the capital/labor ratio of the remaining workers, or the firm may find it advantageous to lay off all the workers and move operations elsewhere.

The laid-off workers are accustomed to a certain level of income and probably expect to achieve something close to that level at the next job they take. In other words, they have a high reservation wage. The reservation wage is the minimum wage that workers will accept. At any wage below his or her reservation wage, the worker will choose unemployment rather than employment. Because of this high reservation wage, such workers are unlikely to take the first job that comes along, especially if they are collecting unemployment benefits. They will instead hold out, hoping to get a job that pays their reservation wage, and they will adjust this reservation wage downward slowly. Such unemployed workers compete less vigorously for jobs and exert less competitive pressure on wage rates. Thus, their unemployment reduces the effectiveness of overall unemployment in controlling inflation and increases the NAIRU.

Union pressure on relative wages thus increases the NAIRU in at least two ways. First, it directly increases the number of unemployed workers by increasing the relative cost of workers and making it more profitable for firms to use fewer workers or move. Second, by increasing unemployed workers' reservation wage, it reduces the effectiveness of any given level of unemployment.

Summary

To review, anything that reduces the feasible real wage that can be achieved in an economy without, at the same time, reducing the target real wage of workers will lead to an increase in the NAIRU. Factors that may reduce the feasible real wage include increases in business costs, reductions in productivity growth, and increases in taxes.

Anything that increases workers' target real wage without increasing the feasible real wage will also increase the NAIRU. Factors that increase workers' target real wage include unemployment benefits and welfare, mismatch, and excessive union pressure on wages.

Phelps's New Theory

Before concluding this chapter on economic theory relating to the NAIRU, we must mention the recent work of Edmund S. Phelps.[14] In a 1994 book, Phelps attempts the monumental task of virtually rewriting macroeconomic theory. He presents an alternative to classical economics, Keynesian economics, and neoclassical economics.

The model and theory are much too complicated to discuss in any detail here, but this new theory, called modern equilibrium theory, agrees with our very simple model on several important points. Factors such as productivity growth, taxes, oil price shocks, and social welfare expenditures are part of Phelps's theory and can potentially cause the NAIRU to rise. This is not to argue, however, that the model used in this book is just a simpler version of Phelps's modern equilibrium theory. The two do not emphasize the same things, and important differences exist.

One of these important differences is Phelps's emphasis on real-world interest rates. In his empirical tests of the modern equilibrium theory, Phelps finds that one of the most important explanations for a high NAIRU is the high level of real-world interest rates, and these high real interest rates are more than partially the result of the high level of world public debt. Many economic models and theories have noted that high real interest rates can push unemployment up. One of Phelps's contributions is to establish linkages between real interest rates and employment and to emphasize world, not just domestic, real interest rates.

In the coming months and years, Phelps's new theory will be much discussed and analyzed. For our purposes here, this new weighty theory adds support to the notion that a NAIRU exists and that tools exist that can be used to reduce it.

THE REST OF THE BOOK

In the rest of the book, the various factors discussed in this chapter that can and perhaps have caused the NAIRU to increase in the United States are analyzed. In Chapter 3, mismatch unemployment is discussed. This is currently perhaps the most popular explanation of the high average level of unemployment in the industrialized countries. It was emphasized at the 1994 Jobs Summit held at President Clinton's request in Detroit. But this diagnosis may very well be wrong. In Chapter 4, attention is focused on factors that may have caused business costs to increase without a compensating increase in productivity. These factors include such things as the oil price shocks and increases in government regulations. In Chapter 5, unemployment insurance and other social welfare programs that may increase the NAIRU are analyzed. In Chapter 6, the effect unions have on wages and fringe benefits is examined. Other analysts have argued that unions have significantly increased the NAIRU in other countries. What about the United States? In Chapter 7, an examination is made of the effect unions have had on productivity growth and, more important, the effect current U.S. labor law has had on productivity growth. Chapter 8 takes a more general look at productivity growth and the NAIRU. Chapter 9 concludes with a summary and review. Each of the chapters presents a few public policy ideas that may help the United States to reduce its NAIRU.

NOTES

1. Robert J. Gordon, *Macroeconomics*, 4th ed. (Boston: Little, Brown, 1987), Appendix A.

2. Stuart E. Weiner, "New Estimates of the Natural Rate of Unemployment," *Federal Reserve Bank of Kansas City Economic Review* 78 (Fourth Quarter 1993), pp. 53-69.

3. The estimates of NAIRU's upper and lower bands are from Stuart E. Weiner, "The Natural Rate of Unemployment: Concepts and Issues," *Federal Reserve Bank of Kansas City Economic Review* 71 (January 1986), pp. 11-24. Weiner estimates these upper and lower bands from eight series on the natural unemployment rate published by different authors.

4. Amanda Bennett, "Business and Academia Clash over a Concept: 'Natural' Jobless Rate," *Wall Street Journal*, January 24, 1995, p. 1.

5. Richard K. Vedder and Lowell E. Gallaway, *Out of Work: Unemployment and Government in Twentieth-Century America* (New York: Holmes & Meier, 1993).

6. See, for example, Michael Bruno and Jeffrey D. Sachs, *Economics of Worldwide Stagflation* (Cambridge, MA: Harvard University Press, 1985); George E. Johnson and Richard Layard, "The Natural Rate of Unemployment: Explanation and Policy," in O. Ashenfelter and R. Layard (eds.), *Handbook of Labor Economics, Volume 2* (New York: Elsevier Science, 1986), Chapter 16; Lawrence H. Summers, *Understanding Unemployment* (Cambridge: MIT Press, 1990).

7. *Wall Street Journal*, January 24, 1995, p. 1.

8. A. William Phillips, "The Relation between Unemployment and the Rate of Change of Money Wage Rates in the United Kingdom, 1861-1957," *Economica* 25 (1958), pp. 283-99.

9. Milton Friedman, "The Role of Monetary Policy," *American Economic Review* 58 (March 1968), pp. 1-17 and Edmund Phelps, "Phillips Curve, Expectations of Inflation, and Optimal Unemployment over Time," *Economica*, n.s., 34 (August 1976), pp. 254-81.

10. Ellen R. Rissman, "What Is the Natural Rate of Unemployment," *Federal Reserve Bank of Chicago Economic Perspectives* 10 (September/October 1986), pp. 3-17.

11. For a more complete discussion, see Richard Layard, *How to Beat Unemployment* (Oxford, England: Oxford University Press, 1986).

12. Ibid.

13. Ibid.

14. Edmund S. Phelps, *Structural Slumps: The Modern Equilibrium Theory of Unemployment, Interest, and Assets* (Cambridge: Harvard University Press, 1994).

CHAPTER 3

A FAULTY DIAGNOSIS OF
UNEMPLOYMENT

In March 1994 a conference involving the finance, labor, commerce, and economics ministers of the G-7 nations (Britain, Canada, France, Germany, Italy, Japan, and the United States) was held at President Clinton's request in Detroit, Michigan. The conference's purpose was to give the ministers a chance to discuss their countries' serious unemployment problems so that they might better understand the causes and cures of high unemployment. The conference became known as the jobs summit.

No doubt exists that unemployment has become more of a problem among the G-7 nations over the last two or three decades. During the period from 1965 to 1975, the average unemployment rate among the G-7 nations was only 3.4 percent. During the period from 1980 to 1990, the average unemployment rate for the G-7 nations was 7.5 percent. Something has obviously gone wrong. What did the jobs summit conclude?

The skimpy published reports available after the jobs summit indicate that the ministers briefly discussed many items, including the role of the private sector in creating jobs, making employment more attractive than welfare, sound macroeconomic policies, the importance of small and medium-sized companies, international trade, and the importance of productivity gains that accompany technological advances. But, according to U.S. Treasury Secretary Lloyd Bentsen, "the need to improve the education, training, and skills of our work forces was central" to the discussions of the ministers at the jobs summit.[1] This fits with the hype that preceded the conference[2] and with President Clinton's March 14, 1994, remarks to open the conference.[3] Put simply, ministers at the jobs summit seem to have concluded that most of the increase in the NAIRU within the G-7 nations has been caused by a growing mismatch between job skills demanded and job skills available. This mismatch, it is surmised, can best be resolved through education and training programs.

Is the high NAIRU of Europe and America really due to an increase in mismatch unemployment? The arguments of this chapter indicate that our government leaders may not really understand unemployment, and they may, at best, be emphasizing the wrong things and, at worst, have failed to grasp the real causes and cures of our high NAIRU.

WHAT COULD HAVE CAUSED MISMATCH UNEMPLOYMENT TO INCREASE?

The economic literature identifies several factors that could have caused mismatch unemployment to increase during the period from 1960 to 1990. In the following paragraphs we look critically at three of them: changes in the demographic composition of the labor force, regional mismatch, and skill mismatch.

Demographics

The changing demographic composition of the labor force may have an important effect on the unemployment rate. A demographic shift in the labor force can cause the NAIRU to increase if the labor force after the demographic shift contains a higher proportion of individuals prone to be unemployed than before the demographic shift. For instance, Ellen Rissman has argued that the increase in the proportion of females, non-whites, and young people in the labor force in the 1970s relative to the 1960s resulted in a small increase in the unemployment rate (basically, because the relative weighting of their higher unemployment rates increased). She argues that at the peak of the demographic shift in 1975, the changing demographics of the labor force contributed around three-quarters of a percentage point to the overall unemployment rate.[4]

How can this effect by measured? Rissman measures the effect by comparing the actual unemployment rate with what economists call a fixed-weight unemployment rate. The fixed-weight unemployment rate computes what the unemployment rate would have been if the demographic composition of the labor force had remained as it was in the selected base period.

Analysts like Rissman have used this methodology to argue that demographic shifts have caused the unemployment rate to increase by a relatively small amount, less than 1 percent. Others have argued that demographic shifts have played a larger role. Robert Gordon, for instance, has argued that most, if not all, of the increase in the unemployment rate between 1954 and 1979 was caused by the changing demographic composition of the labor force.[5]

Still other analysts have argued that demographic shifts have played little, if any, role in the increase in unemployment. Lawrence H. Summers has pointed out that most analysts looking at the effect of changes in labor force composition on the unemployment rate make adjustments for age and sex only. He argues that other changes, like education and primary industry, have also affected labor force composition. After calculating fixed-weight unemployment rates with adjustments for age, sex, marital status, schooling, and primary industry, Summers finds that taking into account the changing composition of the labor force cannot explain the increase in the U.S. unemployment rate.[6] In other words, Summers's methodology seems to show that demographic change cannot explain the increasing NAIRU.

The proportion of women and young people in the labor force definitely increased between 1960 and 1980. In 1956, women of all ages and men under the age of 25 accounted for 41.1 percent of the labor force. By 1979, this was up to 55.1 percent. Summers's analysis, however, makes it problematic to attribute much of the increase in the NAIRU to this fact. In addition, many analysts have pointed out that changes in the composition of the labor force since 1979 should have improved the unemployment picture, but the NAIRU has not returned to its 1960s level.[7]

What can we conclude from the research on demographics and unemployment? In theory, changing demographics can definitely cause the NAIRU to increase. Many analysts attribute at least part of the increase in the NAIRU to demographic factors. The research of other analysts, however, casts doubt on the demographic explanation of rising unemployment. In view of these facts, no definitive statement regarding demographic change and rising unemployment can be made.

Regional Mismatch

Structural unemployment could also result from regional mismatch. In other words, available jobs may be in one region while workers to fill those jobs are located in another region. Some analysts have argued that regional mismatch has increased in the United States as jobs have moved from the Rust Belt to the Sun Belt. George Johnson, for instance, argues that there has been a dramatic shift of economic activity in the United States away from the Rust Belt states toward the Sun Belt states.[8] Casual evidence of this phenomenon comes from differences in regional unemployment rates. For instance, the average unemployment rate in four typical Rust Belt states (New York, Pennsylvania, Ohio, and Michigan) was close to 12 percent in the recession year 1982. The average unemployment rate in four typical Sun Belt states (North Carolina, South Carolina, Georgia, and Florida) was less than 9 percent in that same year.

In order for regional mismatch to explain the increasing U.S. unemployment rate, the regional disparity between unemployment rates must have worsened during the period when the unemployment rate was increasing. Figure 3.1 shows the difference between the unemployment rates in four Rust Belt states and four Sun Belt states during the period from 1960 to 1990. The figure shows that in the early 1960s, unemployment in Rust Belt states was about one percentage point higher than unemployment in Sun Belt states. This difference declined in the late 1960s and then increased dramatically in the recession of 1970. The difference then declined to about the early 1960s level in the mid-1970s, but increased again in the late 1970s and remained at a high level through the 1980-82 recession. The Rust-Belt/Sun-Belt unemployment rate disparity

FIGURE 3.1
THE DIFFERENCE BETWEEN
RUST BELT AND SUN BELT UNEMPLOYMENT*

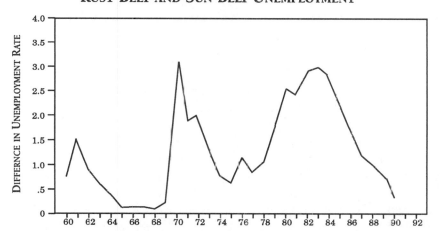

*Source: U.S. Department of Labor, Bureau of Labor Statistics, *Employment and Earnings*, various issues.

declined through most of the 1980s to end up within its 1960s range by 1990.

Changes in the difference between unemployment rates in Rust Belt and Sun Belt states do not seem to be able to explain an unemployment rate that began increasing in the 1960s, continued increasing through the 1970s, and remained at a high level in the 1980s.

Evidence of changes in mobility also does not support the idea that an increase in regional mismatch caused the U.S. unemployment rate to increase. Let us accept the notion that a significant shift in economic activity from the Rust Belt to the Sun Belt has occurred. In order for this shift to increase the unemployment rate, workers who become unemployed in the Rust Belt must be unwilling or unable to move from the depressed region. But an examination of migration rates reveals that people in Rust Belt states were willing and able to move in response to shifting economic activity.

Larry Long's analysis of census data reveals that during the period from 1965 to 1970 the four Rust Belt states that we have called typical had a net out-migration of nearly 1 million people. During the period from 1975 to 1980 an additional 2 million people migrated out of these states. Five of the top six out-migration states in this latter period were Rust Belt states.[9]

Some economic activity may actually have shifted from the Rust Belt to the Sun Belt, but people have apparently been willing to move in response to that shifting activity. Regional mismatch unemployment probably cannot explain much of the increase in the U.S. NAIRU.

Skill Mismatch

Besides the changing demographic composition of the labor force and regional mismatch, another factor that affects the supply of, and demand for, labor and therefore mismatch unemployment is changing skill requirements.

What types of changes or shocks have occurred that could have caused skill mismatch to increase? One of the most widely discussed changes, as already mentioned, is the shift in the industrial structure of the United States. For instance, David Lilien points out that, between 1969 and 1980, manufacturing's share of aggregate employment fell from 28.7 percent to 22.4 percent, a decline of 22.8 percent. During that same time, the share of aggregate employment claimed by retail trade; finance, insurance, and real estate; and service industries grew by 10.1 percent,

14.2 percent, and 23.3 percent respectively. To put things in perspective, manufacturing's share had fallen by only 6.1 percent between 1958 and 1969.[10] Many other authors have argued that the shift from manufacturing jobs to service jobs accelerated during the 1970s and caused significant labor force adjustment problems.

Chinhui Juhn, Kevin Murphy, and Robert Topel conducted an analysis of male unemployment and nonparticipation in the U.S. labor force since 1967.[11] They found that unemployment, nonparticipation, and nonemployment are heavily concentrated among less skilled individuals and that increases in jobless time among the less skilled largely account for the aggregate increases in unemployment. They also argue that shifts in relative labor demand, coupled with declining real-wage levels, account for the increased unemployment among the less skilled. In other words, the less skilled have found that their labor is harder to sell and is worth less in real terms than previously, so they have become unemployed or dropped out of the labor force.

A related argument is that the wave of new technology associated with computerization and microelectronics has caused significant problems of structural adjustment. The computer and microelectronics revolution, it is argued, has fundamentally changed the process of production and the design of products in nearly every branch of the economy. This revolution, it is argued, has not only caused many blue-collar manufacturing jobs to vanish but also cut into the ranks of white-collar workers as fewer clerks and middle managers are needed. Analysts who argue that this revolution has caused significant skill-mismatch problems point out that workers displaced from jobs by a technological revolution may not be quickly rehired. New skills, new attitudes, new forms of organization, new types of capital equipment, new management, and new marketing approaches are needed throughout the economy. While these adjustments take place, unemployment will swell.[12]

Another force that may have contributed to increasing mismatch unemployment, according to Stuart Weiner, is "downsizing" by firms. He argues that many U.S. companies have been aggressively trimming their work forces in recent years. The laid-off workers, often white collar and middle-aged, seem to have had a hard time finding employment and may contribute to a high unemployment rate.[13]

While disagreement over skill-mismatch unemployment is at times intense in the economics profession, the idea that the industrial shift, as well as the computer and microelectronics revolution, has caused significant structural adjustment problems is very widespread. A writer in *The*

New Palgrave: A Dictionary of Economics went so far as to argue that a 1985 publication of a study by the Organization for Economic Cooperation and Development (OECD) marked some degree of consensus that the wave of new technology has raised important problems of structural adjustment. In fact, the idea that a significant level of skill-mismatch unemployment exists has been so widely accepted that almost all countries have initiated special training and retraining programs.[14]

In spite of this widespread acceptance, the empirical evidence on skill-mismatch unemployment is mixed. Stuart Weiner, for one, finds evidence of skill mismatch, but his methodology is not very precise. He inserts dummy variables into his unemployment equations in an attempt to ascertain whether or not structural change occurred in the U.S. economy during three distinct periods, 1961-72, 1973-79, and 1980-93. His estimates seem to indicate that structural change did occur and that structural unemployment has and is contributing to a high unemployment rate. Weiner argues that structural problems like continued defense cutbacks, continued white-collar displacement, and continued skill mismatch may lead to an even higher unemployment rate in the future.[15]

In 1991, Cambridge University published a volume entitled *Mismatch and Labour Mobility*. This volume, the result of a conference held in Venice in January 1990, included 12 papers on the subject of structural unemployment. In summarizing the papers presented at the conference and included in the volume (as well as one paper that was not part of the conference or the volume), Katharine G. Abraham argues that, taken as a whole, the papers provide only very weak evidence of increases in skill mismatch.[16] Within individual countries, findings concerning skill mismatch appear to be sensitive to the measure used and to the occupational groupings employed in the analysis. In other words, one analyst may find empirical evidence of skill mismatch using a particular measurement technique and defining occupational groupings in a particular way, while another analyst using another technique and defining occupational groupings in a broader (or narrower) way may find no evidence. Abraham continues by arguing that the results of the papers on skill mismatch are so fragile that it is difficult to place much confidence in them.

An analysis of the so-called Beveridge curve may help us gain a clearer picture of whether or not an increase in mismatch unemployment, including skill mismatch, has occurred in the United States. The Beveridge curve relates the unemployment rate to the vacancy rate. If the unemployment rate is high and/or increasing, we would expect to see a low and/or decreasing vacancy rate. This is because if firms are laying off workers, and, in general, the demand for labor is relatively weak, it is unlikely that firms will have very many unfilled vacancies. But if the unemployment rate is low and/or decreasing, and thus labor is in relatively short supply, we would expect that the vacancy rate to be relatively high and/or increasing. In this case, unemployed workers are scarce, so many vacancies go unfilled. In other words, we would expect a downward sloping relationship between the unemployment rate and the vacancy rate. If mismatch is a problem, however, we may see high unemployment rates and high vacancies rates occurring at the same time. Although many workers may be available to work, they may not have the skills to fill the existing vacancies. If mismatch is increasing over time, we would expect to see an upward shift in the downward sloping Beveridge curve.

Has the relationship between the U.S. unemployment rate and vacancy rate changed, indicating an increase in mismatch unemployment? Figure 3.2 presents the unemployment rate and a proxy for the vacancy rate for the period from 1957 to 1993. The vacancy rate proxy is derived from the Conference Board's Index of Help Wanted Advertising. This index is an employment-weighted average of the number of help wanted

FIGURE 3.2
**U.S. UNEMPLOYMENT RATE AND
PROXIED VACANCY RATE, 1957-93***

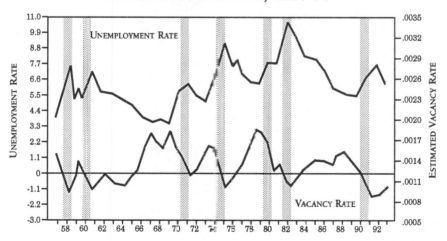

*Sources: Department of Labor, Bureau of Labor Statistics, *Employment and Earnings*, various issues and U.S. Department of Commerce, Bureau of Economic Analysis, *Survey of Current Business*, various issues.

advertisements in 51 major metropolitan newpapers, deflated so that 1967 equals 100. Dividing the national help wanted index by total nonagricultural payroll employment yields a reasonable proxy for the job vacancy rate.[17] We can use this proxy to analyze changes in the vacancy rate. The shaded areas in the figure indicate recessionary periods.

The figure shows that an upward shift in the Beveridge curve has not occurred. In other words, the United States has not seen increasing unemployment rates accompanied by increasing vacancy rates. This fact is also depicted using a different type of chart. Figure 3.3 contains a scatterplot of a three-year average of U.S. unemployment rates (vertical axis) versus a three-year average of the described vacancy rate proxy (horizontal axis) for the period from 1957 to 1993. The figure shows the expected downward sloping curve with no evidence of an upward shift in the curve.

FIGURE 3.3
**SCATTERPLOT OF U.S. UNEMPLOYMENT RATE
VERSUS PROXIED VACANCY RATE, 1957-93***

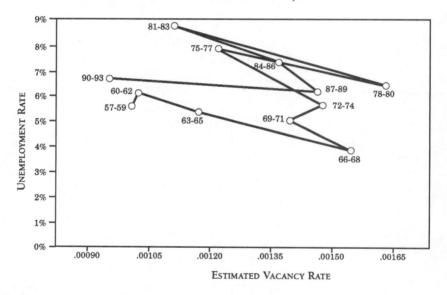

*Each point represents a three-year average. Sources: Department of Labor, Bureau of Labor Statistics, *Employment and Earnings*, various issues and U.S. Department of Commerce, Bureau of Economic Analysis, *Survey of Current Business*, various issues.

If we were to look just at the period from the 1950s to the early 1980s, as some previous analysts have done, we might come to the conclusion that a shift in the Beveridge curve did occur, indicating an increase in mismatch unemployment. Inclusion of data covering all of the 1980s and the early 1990s makes this conclusion difficult to support. In order to use shifts in the Beveridge curve as support for the argument that mismatch unemployment has increased, one has to be willing to now argue that structural unemployment has decreased significantly in the late 1980s and early 1990s. Few are willing to accept this argument.

Several recent papers have, in fact, pointed out that the Beveridge curve is really not very useful in analyzing changes in mismatch unemployment. For one thing, shifts in the Beveridge curve are too sudden to be explained by structural changes. In addition, the Beveridge curve suffers from potential aggregation bias problems, and it can shift for reasons unrelated to mismatch or structural phenomena.[18]

Richard Layard, Stephen Nickell, and Richard Jackman have proposed another measure of mismatch unemployment.[19] They ask if there is some simple index by which one could assess how the structure of unemployment is related to its average level. They derive an expression that shows how average unemployment is related to the dispersion of the unemployment rates across sectors. This expression is:

$$\log(u) = \text{constant} + 1/2\text{var}(u_i/u)$$

In other words, the log of the average unemployment rate is equal to some constant plus one-half of the variance of sectoral unemployment rates divided by the average unemployment rate. The minimum level of log unemployment is given by the constant and occurs when unemployment rates have been equalized. But if unemployment rates are unequal, unemployment rises in proportion to $1/2\text{var}(u_i/u)$. Given this equation, the natural index of the structure of unemployment is $1/2\text{var}(u_i/u)$, one-half of the variance of relative unemployment rates. It measures the proportional excess of unemployment over its minimum. It is zero, if in each sector, labor demand bears the same proportion to labor supply.

Figure 3.4 shows the Layard, Nickell, and Jackman mismatch index for the United States from 1964 to 1993. The sectoral unemployment rates (u_i) are, in this case, occupations and the variance of the occupational unemployment rates divided by the average unemployment rate is weighted by nonfarm employment for each occupation. We must note that, beginning in 1982, the Bureau of Labor Statistics changed the way it defines and reports occupational employment and unemployment

FIGURE 3.4
**LAYARD, NICKELL, AND JACKMAN'S MISMATCH INDEX, ONE-HALF
THE VARIANCE OF RELATIVE UNEMPLOYMENT RATES, 1964-93 (THE
SECTORS ARE OCCUPATIONS)***

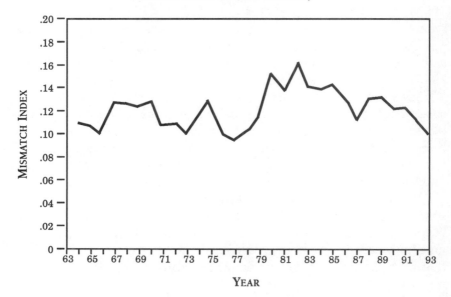

YEAR

* Source: Department of Labor, Bureau of Labor Statistics, *Employment and Earnings*, various issues.

numbers. The numbers after 1982 are, therefore, not strictly comparable to the numbers before 1982. But, since we are interested in the dispersion of unemployment rates and not in any one occupational unemployment rate, we can still use the time series in Figure 3.4 to gain some knowledge about how mismatch has changed.

The figure clearly shows that mismatch on this definition has not increased. Changes in the structure of unemployment cannot, therefore, be used as an explanation of the higher U.S. NAIRU. Layard, Nickell, and Jackman present this same argument not just for the United States but for virtually every other industrialized country. They make one other very important point. Arguing that the increasing NAIRU cannot be attributed to an increase in mismatch does not mean that the *number* of unemployed people who are 'mismatched' has not risen. If unemployment rises for some reason and the proportional mismatch is constant, then the absolute number of mismatched individuals will rise.

So where do we stand with regard to skill-mismatch unemployment? The notion that skill mismatch has worsened and has contributed to a worsening unemployment situation is widespread and widely accepted. Some evidence exists supporting this notion, but strong empirical evidence does not exist even for those countries that are thought to have the worst skill-mismatch problems like Great Britain, let alone for the United States where skill-mismatch problems are thought to be less severe.

A note on the work of Edmund Phelps is in order.[20] Edmund Phelps is the author of a recent book on unemployment entitled *Structural Slumps* which is bound to be much discussed among professional economists. He refers to his unemployment theory in the book as the structuralist theory of unemployment. This does not mean that Phelps believes that some form of mismatch is responsible for the increase in the unemployment rate. In fact, his empirical work says nothing about mismatch, and, by inference, he must believe that an increase in mismatch unemployment cannot explain the increase in the U.S. unemployment rate. What he means by structuralist theory is that his theory is concerned with analyzing not short-run, monetary-induced changes in unemployment, but long-run changes in equilibrium unemployment.

EUROPE AND MISMATCH UNEMPLOYMENT

Lacking strong empirical evidence of mismatch unemployment, perhaps a closer look at an area of the world that has significant unemployment problems will be helpful. Over the 1982-92 decade, unemployment in the European Community averaged 9.9 percent; even during peaks in economic activity, the rate was still more than 9 percent. In contrast, the U.S. unemployment rate averaged 6.8 percent during this period, reaching a low of 5.3 percent in 1989 and never topping 7.5 percent. The European Community obviously has serious unemployment problems. As stated by *The Economist*, "Given such figures, it is absurd to deny that a large part of the EC's [European Community] unemployment problem is deep-seated and non-cyclical—and that something more imaginative than pumping up aggregate demand is needed to deal with it."[21]

Does skill mismatch explain the woeful performance of European labor markets? As already mentioned, Richard Layard, Stephen Nickell, and Richard Jackman, three economists who wrote a 1991 book that takes a thorough look at unemployment in OECD countries, argue that it does not. They conclude that "the unconditional payment of benefits for an indefinite period is clearly a major cause of high European unemployment."[22] *The Economist* points out the same thing: "Europe's long history of shamefully high unemployment shows that its labour markets are broken, and need to be fixed. A chief cause—especially of the rising toll of long-term unemployment—is welfare benefits that are too generous for too long, and which place too few demands on recipients to find a new job."[23]

This explanation makes sense intuitively. Europe has obviously had a much worse unemployment record than has the United States. Europe, without question, has had much more generous unemployment and welfare benefits than has the United States. But both Europe and the United States have been subject to the industrial shift and the microelectronics revolution that are said to be behind the increase in mismatch unemployment. If mismatch were the major cause of an increasing unemployment rate, then the U.S. unemployment experience should more closely match the European one than it does.

This is not to argue that we should ignore people who become unemployed because of shifts in industrial structure or changes in technology. Nor does the argument imply that policies designed to combat mismatch unemployment, like training and retraining programs, do no good. But the evidence reviewed in this chapter, suggesting that skill mismatch may not be the major cause of rising unemployment, suggests that we cannot expect major investments in such policies to reduce unemployment significantly. In fact, as argued in a later chapter, excessive government assistance to the unemployed probably increases unemployment.

CONCLUSIONS AND RECOMMENDATIONS

Can we blame mismatch unemployment for the increase in the NAIRU? While many have pointed to changing demographics, increasing regional mismatch, and/or increasing skill mismatch as major causes of increasing unemployment, evidence does not yet provide strong support for any of these having caused our current unemployment problems.

Demographic change has definitely occurred bringing more youth, women, and nonwhites into the labor force. These groups typically have higher turnover and higher within-group unemployment rates. Increasing their relative weighting within the labor force should increase the NAIRU. But other demographic changes have also occurred, and when these other changes are taken into account, the effect of demographic change on the NAIRU does not appear great.

Shifts in regional economic activity have also definitely occurred. But evidence from regional differences in unemployment rates and migration rates does not support the notion that increasing regional mismatch has caused the NAIRU to increase.

Finally, several factors may have caused skill mismatch to increase, including changes in industrial structure, shifts in relative labor demand, introduction of new technologies, and others. In spite of the popularity of arguments that rely on this diagnosis of the increasing NAIRU, little empirical evidence exists to support it.

If this faulty diagnosis simply caused a few papers to be published in academic journals, then little harm would be done. But the faulty diagnosis is not just of academic interest. It leads to policies and programs that cannot reduce the NAIRU because they are based on a faulty diagnosis of the problem. It is to such policies and programs that we now turn.

Training and Education

On March 9, 1994, the Clinton administration unveiled its Reemployment Act of 1994. The act seeks to "transform our current unemployment system into a system that promotes reemployment by consolidating the existing myriad of training programs, providing easy access to job training and job search services at nationwide one-stop shopping centers, and by creating a system that promotes lifelong learning."[24] The new system is mainly the brainchild of Labor Secretary Robert Reich, and it is based on the current German unemployment system.

The German system may not, however, be a system the United States wants to emulate. The German unemployment rate has been much higher than the U.S. unemployment rate for a number of years. In addition, their job creation rate has been dismal when compared to that of the United States. Their state-run training and retraining programs definitely promote training. If we were to measure the success of their program in terms of training provided, then it could be labeled nothing but a success. But the workers are often trained for jobs that don't exist by state bureaucrats who do not understand what the market really needs. In addition, the program is so expensive that potential employers cannot afford to hire additional workers and pay the high tax rates at the same time. Unemployment payments are so generous that unemployed workers have little incentive to go back to work. It is ironic that just as Reich was writing his program based on the German model, Germany was moving in the opposite direction—privatizing part of the functions of its job centers.[25]

Before he became president, Bill Clinton promised to impose a 1.5 percent payroll tax on companies with more than 50 workers that don't spend at least that much on training. This proposed policy was also obviously the brainchild of Labor Secretary Robert Reich, who previously recommended a 2.5 percent payroll tax.[26]

Justifying such a policy on the basis of reducing the U.S. unemployment rate is, however, problematic. First, as pointed out by *Fortune* magazine's Myron Magnet, such a tax would probably increase unemployment. "If labor costs suddenly zoom up by 1.5 percent and employers, facing stiff global competition, can't easily raise prices, they're likely to stop hiring, freeze wages, and perhaps even lay people off."[27] The effect of a government- mandated training program, the cost of which is borne by companies, could very well be to raise employment costs, depress take-home wages, and inhibit job creation, thus harming the group that supposedly is being helped.

It is hard to disagree with the notion that better-trained workers are good for the economy and good for the nation. Robert Reich's 1991 book *The Work of Nations* makes this point quite persuasively.[28] If the United States is to thrive as a nation and provide a decent standard of living for its citizens, it must be able to compete in the worldwide marketplace for skilled labor. Analysts, however, do not all agree that the way to accomplish this task is to require employers to spend x amount of dollars on training. Evidence exists that the way to compete in a world that requires skilled, problem-solving, self-disciplined workers is to build a school system that provides such workers. This is not to underestimate the importance of on-the-job training. Primary and secondary school systems cannot provide every employer with every type of worker needed, and employers realize that they are going to have to provide the specific training needed for their specific jobs. What employers want are trainable workers. They want workers who can read and write and solve simple mathematical problems; workers who exhibit a willingness to show up on time and work hard; workers who are confident in their ability to learn new skills, who know how to learn and are willing to learn. Above all employers want workers with strong personal values like responsibility and honesty, in other words, employees who know how to take responsibility for, and pride in, their work and who will put in an honest day's work for an honest day's pay.

In a 1988 paper entitled "The Skills Employers Want," Anthony P.

Carnevale, Leila J. Gainer, Ann S. Meltzer, and Shari L. Holland argue that today's employers need workers with good basic reading, writing, and computational skills, but they also need other basic skills that our educational system can help provide. These other basic skills include the following:[29]

- learning to learn—the ability to acquire the knowledge and skills needed to learn effectively, no matter what the learning situation
- listening—the ability to heed the key points of customers', suppliers', and co-workers' concerns
- oral communications—the ability to convey an adequate response to those concerns
- problem solving—the ability to think on one's feet
- creative thinking—the ability to come up with innovative solutions
- self-esteem—the ability to have pride in oneself and believe in one's potential to be successful
- goal-setting/motivation—the ability to know how to get things done
- personal and career development skills—the awareness of the skills needed to perform well in the work place
- interpersonal skills—the ability to get along with customers, suppliers, and coworkers
- teamwork—the ability to work with others to achieve a goal
- negotiation—the ability to build consensus through give-and-take
- organizational effectiveness—the understanding of where the organization is headed and how one can make a contribution
- leadership—the ability to assume responsibility and motivate coworkers when necessary

Robert Reich's work correctly focuses attention on the fact that our nation prospers only when our workers prosper, and our workers will prosper only if they can compete with workers in other countries on the basis of skill and productivity. The logical conclusion to Reich's analysis is that we must demand and build a world-class education system that provides the basic skills needed by today's employers.

Robert Reich's book is not about education reform, yet he writes a great deal about the U.S. education system and the need for reform. This book also is not about education reform, but a discussion of worker skills would be incomplete without a brief discussion of reforming the U.S. education system.

To put this discussion in context, let us again mention the facts about skill-mismatch unemployment. First, the idea that a significant level of skill mismatch unemployment exists is widespread and widely accepted. Second, while some casual evidence of skill-mismatch unemployment exists, little empirical support can be found. Given this lack of strong empirical support, it would seem foolhardy to embark on a major program of training and retraining. If skill-mismatch unemployment is not a major cause of our unemployment problem, such a program would do little good and much harm in terms of wasted taxpayer dollars and further eroded confidence in the ability of our government to solve any problem. But these arguments do not mean that we should sit back and let businesses worry about the skill level of our labor force. We cannot deny that our country's well-being depends, to a large extent, on its human capital. An educated, disciplined, trainable workforce will attract global businesses and capital and help insulate the economy from any future changes or shocks that might cause skill-mismatch unemployment. These are not the only reasons we must insist on a world-class educational system, but they are powerful ones.

Now, some well-known statistics about education. American children, as a whole, are behind their counterparts in Canada, Japan, Sweden, and Britain in mathematical proficiency, science, and geography.[30] All too many U.S. students emerge from school functionally illiterate. In fact, one study argues that 17 percent of our 17-year-olds are functionally illiterate.[31] A report by the American Society for Training and Development and the U.S. Department of Labor points out that U.S. employers are increasingly reliant on the skills of employees for improvements in efficiency and quality, customer service, and the development of new applications for existing products and services. Yet, this increasing reliance on human capital is on a collision course with the emerging demographic reality in the United States: "The quantity of human resources available for entry-level jobs is declining. Moreover, the quality of entry-level employees is declining as more and more young workers are drawn from populations with insufficient human capital investments prior to work."[32]

What can we do about this dismal situation? The answer presented here is not that of Robert Reich. He recommends more federal involvement and spending more money. This book suggests that the federal government usually opts for one-best solutions and that these often end up being heavily bureaucratic and inefficient.[33] One of the principal criticisms of our present school systems is that they are already too bureaucratic. Perhaps a better solution is to (1) allow states to compete in building good schools and (2) force schools to compete for students. In other words, institute a system of choice where parents and students must actively choose the type of school that they will attend, and schools must provide a quality product or simply go out of business.

This book is not a tome on education reform or school choice. These subjects are addressed at length by other authors in other books. Our recommendation on school choice is made because our present system is not working, we do not need a new bureaucracy, and we do not need to throw more money into the old one. We need a new system. A system based on competition between independent producers is, every day, proving capable of providing quality products at reasonable prices. In addition, the market provides the right product—in other words, the product that consumers want. Surely, we can use this powerful tool (the market), which has proven itself against socialist systems, to help in our task of providing students with a quality education and employers with work-ready, trainable employees. Such an education system is a condition necessary to reduce the high U.S. unemployment rate.

One great advantage that a choice system has over the traditional state-run, bureaucratic system is that it emphasizes personal responsibility. As stated earlier, employers want, most of all, responsible employees. A system of choice teaches such responsibility. Students and their parents are responsible to choose schools that will help them accomplish their personal goals. No longer will we be able to blame "the system" for educational failure, because under a choice system we are responsible to choose the right school, and we must (and will) demand, as consumers, that the schools we choose deliver the right product.

Many foes of a choice system of education seem to believe that parents are incapable of properly directing the education of their children. This is arrogant in the extreme and has shades of "Big Brother." Many also argue that a choice system will hurt the disadvantaged and the poor. If our system stops telling disadvantaged kids and their parents that they are victims of the system and starts telling them that they are responsible for their own failures and successes in life and then gives them the opportunity to make their own choices and be responsible, we may just find out that even the disadvantaged are capable of learning and growing and overcoming. This is the American dream—to live in a land of opportunity and to take advantage of that opportunity. Right now we are depriving many thousands of this dream and allowing the education and other social welfare systems to tell them that they are victims and are neither able nor responsible to do anything about their situation.

NOTES

1. *Summary Statement of Treasury Secretary Lloyd Bentsen on Behalf of the G-7 Jobs Conference, Detroit, Michigan* (Washington, DC: White House, Office of the Press Secretary, March 15, 1994).

2. For instance, Steven Greenhouse, "Clinton Plan for Unemployment Conference Is Aimed at Stirring Up Public Support," *New York Times,* July 10, 1993, p. 39.

3. *Remarks by the President at the G-7 Jobs Conference, Fox Theater, Detroit, Michigan* (Washington, DC: White House, Office of the Press Secretary, March 14, 1994).

4. Ellen R. Rissman, "What Is the Natural Rate of Unemployment?" *Federal Reserve Bank of Chicago Economic Perspectives* 10 (September/October 1986), pp. 3-17.

5. Robert J. Gordon, *Macroeconomics, 4th ed.* (Boston: Little, Brown, 1987). Gordon was talking about the increase in the "natural rate of unemployment," which excludes cyclical unemployment.

6. Lawrence H. Summers, *Understanding Unemployment* (Cambridge: MIT Press, 1990).

7. For example, Keith M. Carlson, "How Much Lower Can the Unemployment Rate Go?" *Federal Reserve Bank of St. Louis Review* 70 (July/August 1988), pp. 44-57.

8. George E. Johnson, "Do We Know Enough about the Unemployment Problem To Know What, If Anything, Will Help?" in D. Lee Bawden and Felicity Skidmore (eds.), *Rethinking Employment Policy* (Washington, DC: Urban Institute Press, 1989), pp. 37-57.

9. Larry Long, *Migration and Residential Mobility in the United States* (New York: Russell Sage Foundation, 1988).

10. David M. Lilien, "Sectoral Shifts and Cyclical Unemployment," *Journal of Political Economy* 90 (1982), pp. 777-93.

11. Chinhui Juhn, Kevin M. Murphy, and Robert H. Topel, "Why Has the Natural Rate of Unemployment Increased over Time?" *Brookings Papers on Economic Activity* 2 (1991), pp. 75-126.

12. For example, Luc Soete and Christopher Freeman, "New Technologies, Investment and Employment Growth," in Organization for Economic Co-operation and Development, *Employment Growth and Structural Change* (Paris: OECD, 1985), pp. 52-83.

13. Stuart E. Weiner, "New Estimates of the Natural Rate of Unemployment," *Federal Reserve Bank of Kansas City Economic Review* 78 (Fourth Quarter 1993), pp. 53-69.

14. John Eatwell, Murray Milgate, and Peter Newman, *The New Palgrave: A*

Dictionary of Economics (New York: Macmillan, 1987).

15. Weiner, "New Estimates."

16. Katharine G. Abraham, "Mismatch and Labour Mobility: Some Final Remarks," in Fiorella Podoa Schioppa (ed.), *Mismatch and Labour Mobility* (New York: Cambridge University Press, 1991), pp. 453-85.

17. Katharine G. Abraham and Lawrence F. Katz, "Cyclical Unemployment: Sectoral Shifts or Aggregate Disturbances?" *Journal of Political Economy* 94 (1986), pp. 507-22.

18. See Olivier Jean Blanchard and Peter Diamond, "The Beveridge Curve," *Brookings Papers on Economic Activity* 1 (1989), pp. 1-60; Comments accompanying Blanchard and Diamond, *Brookings Papers on Economic Activity* 1 (1989), pp. 61-76; Axel H. Borsch-Supan, "Panel Data Analysis of the Beveridge Curve: Is There a Macroeconomic Relation between the Rate of Unemployment and the Vacancy Rate?" *Economic* 58 (August 1991), pp. 279-97; and Wolfgang Franz (ed.), *Structural Unemployment* (New York: Springer-Verlag, 1992).

19. Richard Layard, Stephen Nickell, and Richard Jackman, *Unemployment: Macroeconomic Performance and the Labour Market* (Oxford, England: Oxford University Press, 1991), Chapter 6.

20. Edmund S. Phelps, *Structural Slumps: The Modern Equilibrium Theory of Unemployment, Interest, and Assets* (Cambridge: Harvard University Press, 1994).

21. *The Economist*, June 26, 1993, p. 17.

22. Layard, Nickell, and Jackman, *Unemployment: Macroeconomic Performance and the Labour Market*, p. 62.

23. *The Economist*, June 26, 1993, p. 17.

24. "Profiling and Job Search Assistance," in *The G-7 Jobs Conference, Detroit, Michigan, March 14-15, 1994: Innovative Ideas That Work* (Washington, DC: The White House, Office of the Press Secretary), p. 5.

25. Amity Shales, "Re-Employment that Kills Jobs," *Wall Street Journal*, April 26, 1994, p. .

26. Robert B. Reich, "Training a Skilled Work Force: Why U.S. Corporations Neglect Their Workers," *Dissent* (Winter 1992), pp. 42-46.

27. Myron Magnet, "Why Job Growth Is Stalled," *Fortune*, March 8, 1993, p. 57.

28. Robert B. Reich, *The Work of Nations: Preparing Ourselves for 21st Century Capitalism* (New York: Vintage Books, 1992).

29. Anthony P. Carnevale, Leila J. Gainer, Ann S. Meltzer, and Shari L. Holland, "The Skills Employers Want," *Training and Development Journal* 42 (October 1988), pp. 22-30.

30. A large number of surveys have documented the standing of U.S. stu-

dents compared to students in other countries, for example, "U.S. Students Near the Foot of the Class," *Science*, March 1988, p. 237.

31. *National Assessment of Educational Progress*, various issues.

32. Anthony P. Carnevale and Leila J. Gainer, *The Learning Enterprise* (Washington, DC: American Society for Training and Development and the U.S. Department of Labor, 1989), p. 4.

33. Garry K. Ottosen, *Making American Government Work: A Proposal to Reinvigorate Federalism* (Lanham, MD: University Press of America, 1992).

CHAPTER 4

BUSINESS COSTS, GOVERNMENT REGULATIONS, AND THE NAIRU

As discussed in Chapter 2, the jobs summit centered on skill mismatch as the principal culprit in Europe's and America's high unemployment. Improved training and retraining programs are the logical response to such a malady. The chapter concluded that that diagnosis may very well be wrong. It was suggested that the available evidence cannot be used to justify major increases in training and retraining programs. Improved education is a must. However, spending billions of dollars on education and training programs that will not accomplish their goals will only further erode confidence in our government.

If the jobs summit focused on the wrong things, then what are the major causes of the increased NAIRU among the G-7 nations and, more specifically, in the United States? The search in this chapter begins at one of the most basic levels—an analysis of business costs.

How can business costs affect the NAIRU? Increases in business costs that do not somehow increase productivity are ultimately passed on to consumers in the form of higher prices. These price increases get built into various cost-of-living measures like the Consumer Price Index (CPI). Increases in prices lead to increases in wages either through formal wage indexation to the CPI or more informally through demands for wage increases to keep up with inflation. As wages increase, businesses again experience increased costs and raise their prices again. Inflation begins to rear its ugly head. If the cost increases that initiated the inflationary impulse turn out to be permanent and are therefore added to the cost structure of the economy, then businesses, in effect, require more inputs to produce the same level of output. Productivity by definition is reduced.

In order to control inflation, government monetary authorities increase interest rates, which, in turn, cause economic growth to slow and cause slack in the economy to increase. In other words, aggregate demand is reduced. As aggregate demand is reduced, unemployment increases, as do inventories. Upward pressure on prices is reduced, and inflation slows. As discussed in Chapter 1, this method used by government monetary authorities to control inflation is a very expensive tool.

What are the major costs of doing business that could have risen and caused an increase in the U.S. NAIRU? The largest business cost is labor. We will not discuss labor costs here but do discuss them in Chapter 6. Another category of business expenses is materials costs. Trade shocks can increase the NAIRU through their effect on materials costs. The two oil price shocks, as well as other trade shocks that occurred in the 1970s, may have contributed to inflation and thus to an increase in the NAIRU. In this chapter we examine data on material prices to see if increases in this cost of business did, indeed, contribute to an increase in the NAIRU. Yet, another category of business costs is capital equipment and structures. This chapter also briefly examines data on the prices of these items. Finally, businesses have many costs that we simply call "other costs." The most important of these other costs is the cost of government regulations. The costs of government regulation in relation to the U.S. NAIRU are also examined in this chapter.

THE COST OF MATERIALS

Figure 4.1 shows the annual percentage change in producer prices for intermediate materials and fuels. An examination of this figure indicates that the rate of change of both intermediate materials prices and fuel prices increased massively in 1973 with the advent of the first oil shock. The rate of change of intermediate materials prices and fuel prices then declined in 1974 and 1975 but began to increase again in 1978 and 1979 with the advent of the second oil shock.

Figure 4.2 shows the percentage change in the price of crude oil during the period from 1953 to 1991. Figure 4.3 shows the level of crude oil prices over the same period. These two figures clearly show that between the early 1970s and the early 1980s the price of this important commodity increased greatly. This increase may have been important enough to contribute to an increase in the price of nearly all intermediate materials and thus to an increase in the unemployment rate.

FIGURE 4.1
PERCENTAGE CHANGE IN PRODUCER PRICES*

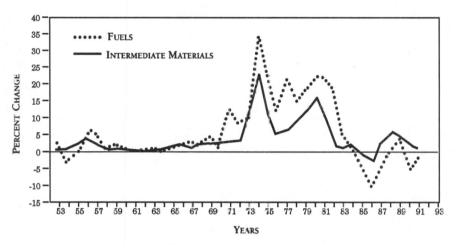

* Source: Department of Labor, Bureau of Labor Statistics, *Producer Prices*, various issues.

FIGURE 4.2
PERCENTAGE CHANGE IN CRUDE OIL, FIRST PURCHASE PRICES*

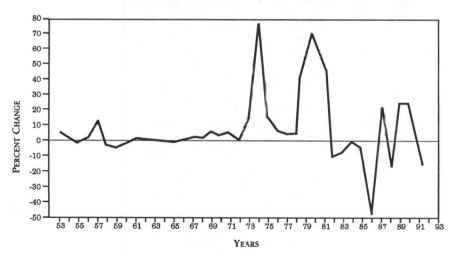

* Source: U.S. Department of Energy, Energy Information Administration, *Annual Energy Review 1991* (June 1992).

FIGURE 4.3
CRUDE OIL, FIRST PURCHASE PRICES*

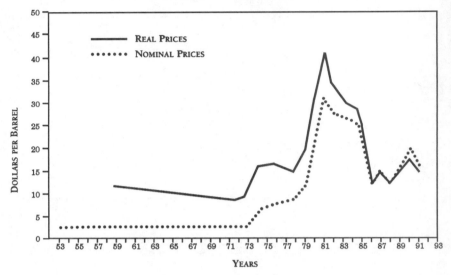

*Source: U.S. Department of Energy, Energy Information Administration, *Annual Energy Review 1991* (June 1992).

The correlation coefficient between changes in the prices of intermediate goods and changes in the prices of fuel is 0.77. Correlation does not necessarily imply causation, but it does lead us to believe that the oft-discussed 1973 and 1979 oil price shocks may have played a role in the increase in material costs. If the oil price shocks helped to increase costs significantly, then they may have contributed to an increase in the U.S. unemployment rate. Edmund Phelps's analysis, for one, definitely cites increased real oil prices as a factor causing unemployment to increase.[1]

The oil price shocks were not the only important events that may have increased material and, thus, business costs during the 1970s. The Nixon administration introduced wage and price controls in August 1971. These controls were loosened in early 1973 and formally abandoned in May 1974. The prices of previously controlled items shot up even before the controls were formally lifted. Severe worldwide crop failures beginning in 1972 also caused prices of many food commodities to skyrocket between mid-1972 and early 1974. For instance, corn prices stood at about $1.40 per bushel in late 1972; by mid-1973 corn was selling at more than $3.40 per bushel. In late 1972, soybeans were selling at about $3.50 per bushel; by mid-1973, the price had reached an astounding $12.90 per bushel. During the same time, wheat increased from $2.20 per bushel to $6.00 per bushel, feeder cattle increased from 38 cents per pound to more than 70 cents per pound, and live hogs increased from 30 cents per pound to more than 60 cents per pound.

The increase in commodity prices combined with the oil price shocks caused the cost of doing business to increase significantly. This inflationary impulse could have been contained without inflation only if workers had been willing to accept an equivalent cut in their real wage. As pointed out by Richard Layard, workers resisted, inflation rose, the government then fought inflation, and unemployment rose.[2] In other words, the oil price shocks and other commodity price increases of the 1970s probably had something to do with the increase in the NAIRU that occurred at that time. The effect, however, could only have been temporary. As Figures 4.1, 4.2, and 4.3 make clear, the rate of increase of oil and other intermediate materials prices declined significantly after 1980. Yet, the NAIRU rate has not returned to the levels that were common previous to the oil price shocks. The conclusion is that while the shocks that occurred during the 1970s may have contributed to the increase in the NAIRU that occurred at that time, something else must also have played a significant role, something that has not yet subsided.

THE COST OF CAPITAL EQUIPMENT AND STRUCTURES

What about the cost of capital equipment and structures? Figure 4.4 (page 56) shows the annual percentage change in capital equipment and construction costs for commercial and factory buildings. The figure reveals that capital equipment costs and construction costs, like materials costs, seem to have increased at nearly the same time as the two oil price shocks. As oil prices increased dramatically in the 1970s, so did capital equipment and construction costs. As oil price increases have declined, so has the rate of increase of capital equipment and construction costs.

The conclusion reached with regard to materials costs and unemployment appears to be applicable here as well. Increases in the costs of capital equipment and construction, which at least coincided with increases in the price of oil and other commodities, may have contributed to an increase in the U.S. NAIRU in the 1970s but cannot explain why it has not declined since that time.

FIGURE 4.4

CHANGE IN CONSTRUCTION AND CAPITAL EQUIPMENT COSTS*

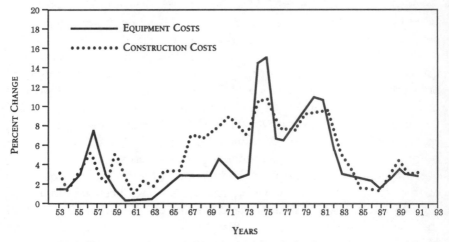

*Source: U.S. Department of Labor, Bureau of Labor Statistics, and U.S. Department of Commerce, *Business Statistics*, 27th Edition (June 1992)

THE COST OF GOVERNMENT REGULATIONS

At the beginning of this chapter we mentioned four categories of business costs that may have an effect on the NAIRU—labor, material, capital equipment and structures, and other costs. Costs due to government regulations are among the most important of the other costs. This section examines government regulations and the associated costs in some detail.

David Vogel has argued that between 1900 and 1980, the United States experienced three sustained political efforts to regulate the economy.[3] The first of these periods is referred to as the Progressive Era. It roughly spans the years between 1902 and 1914. It was an era marked by the expansion of a type of regulation often called economic regulation, which we more clearly define shortly. The second period was the New Deal period. This period began with the inauguration of Franklin Roosevelt (FDR) in the spring of 1933 and was effectively concluded by 1938, the midpoint of FDR's second term. It also involved an expansion of economic regulation.

The third period—which can be called the Social Regulation Era— was rooted in the consumer, civil rights, and antiwar movements that emerged during the 1960s. It was a period marked by the expansion of a type of regulation called social regulation, which we review shortly. Vogel points out that the social regulatory reform effort maintained considerable momentum throughout much of the 1970s with the growth of public concern over the impact of the large corporations on American foreign policy, the physical environment, the safety and health of workers, employment opportunities for women and minorities, the integrity of the political process, the availability of energy, and the stability of the American economy. The Social Regulation Era roughly spans the period from 1964 to 1980.

Economic Regulation

As hinted at in the previous paragraphs, economists typically identify two broad categories of government regulations as applied to business. The first category is called economic regulation. Economic regulatory arrangements share certain common factors.[4] Public authorities first determine that an unacceptable relationship exists between producers and consumers. In response, an agency or independent commission is established to direct the activities of the entire industry. The regulatory authority may set minimum or maximum levels of service, perhaps including price, level of output, entry into, or exit, from the industry, rate of return, and the market to be served. The regulated firms are usually allowed to receive a "fair rate of return" in exchange for being so heavily regulated.

The first federal government use of economic regulation came in 1887, when President Grover Cleveland signed the Interstate Commerce Act. The Interstate Commerce Act created the Interstate Commerce Commission (ICC), the first independent federal regulatory commission. The ICC was empowered to set reasonable railroad rates, protect consumers from price discrimination, force the posting of rates, and prohibit a variety of anticompetitive practices. With commissioners appointed by the president and confirmed by the Senate, the ICC became a model for the structure of future regulatory agencies. Designed to be isolated from political pressures, commission members were given quasi-judicial powers to determine a variety of policies.

Several rationales are used to justify the use of economic regulation. An understanding of these justifications will help in understanding economic regulation. According to Larry N. Gerston, Cynthia Fraleigh, and Robert Schwab, the primary justification is the claim of market failure, a condition that sometimes accompanies the existence of a natural monopoly. A natural monopoly exists when an industry has very high fixed costs in establishing service, so high that it makes economic sense to have no more than one firm offering the service. Electrical service is a typical example. An unregulated firm with a monopoly in electrical services could easily set a price well above the competitive price, and consumers would have little choice but to pay or go without electricity. Economic regulation is, therefore, justified.

A second justification mentioned by Gerston, Fraleigh, and Schwab follows from the perceived need for a central authority to allocate a common resource. For example, the market might create chaos without some means of assigning radio frequencies. Regulation helps ensure that limited common resources are used efficiently and not depleted by one producer to the detriment of society.

A third justification for economic regulation is that certain industries provide basic services that should be available to all. Without regulation, the costs of providing such basic services as power and telephones to remote areas might be prohibitive.

The fourth justification for intervention was especially popular when economic regulation was just beginning. As industries increased in size toward the end of the nineteenth century, competition often became cutthroat. Regulation, it was thought, was needed to prevent such things as price discrimination, price wars, or other unstable conditions.

A fifth justification was, and is, that new and emerging industries need protection and encouragement during vulnerable stages of development. The risky enterprises of aviation and nuclear power were both regulated in this way to ensure their development.

Past regulation, according to Gerston, Fraleigh, and Schwab, has also been used as a justification for new or continuing regulation. By this rationale, once an industry has been placed under federal control, its investors are assumed to have certain property rights. Regulation may thus continue and expand to keep currently regulated firms from suffering losses, thus protecting, as much as regulating, the industry.

Has *economic* regulation expanded significantly in recent years? The simple answer is no. Most of the economic regulation in the United States was enacted during the first two periods of regulatory expansion. In fact, as the twentieth century began, the ICC seemed destined to be the one federal agency that would handle all aspects of economic regulation. But in 1913, Congress established the Federal Reserve Board to regulate the banking industry. In 1927 the Federal Radio Commission (later known as the Federal Communications Commission [FCC]) was established. In the aftermath of the Great Depression, a wave of government regulation was enacted as public confidence in market mechanisms waned. From 1932 to 1934, the financial services industry saw four major new agencies formed to regulate it. With the Motor Carrier Act of 1935, the ICC was allowed to control major segments of the trucking industry, including entry, types of commodities transported, and rates. In 1938, Congress created the Civil Aeronautics Authority, two years later replacing it with the Civil Aeronautics Board, to regulate the civilian aviation industry. Many other regulatory commissions were created as Franklin Roosevelt's New Deal attempted to cope with the Great Depression. According to Gerston, Fraleigh, and Schwab, within a decade, the federal government regulated steamships, airlines, trucks, and trains; telephones, telegraphs, radios, and televisions; pipelines, dams, and electricity; banks, savings-and-loan associations, savings banks, and stock exchanges.[5]

World War II brought to a close the two eras of economic regulation. Although sporadic efforts at economic regulation occurred during the 1960s and 1970s, the changes were minimal compared to those of the first third of the century.

Social Regulation

Whereas the first two episodes of regulatory expansion had been directed toward control of the economic sector, during the third episode, most new regulations were directed toward protecting the environment, consumers, or workers. This type of regulation has been called social regulation to distinguish it from economic regulation.

Let us compare and contrast these two types of regulation. Economic regulation is designed to give governments control over major economic decisions like pricing, rate of return, and entry and exit. It may be applied to all aspects of any particular industry. Social regulation focuses not on particular industries but more narrowly on specific attributes of products and processes. Social regulations cut across many industries. Social regulators have narrow mandates, such as making consumer products safer or the air cleaner, and they are not concerned with any particular industry or segment. Murray L. Weidenbaum has provided the diagram shown in Figure 4.5 to help explain the difference between economic and social regulation.[6]

FIGURE 4.5
WEIDENBAUM'S DIAGRAM ON VARIATIONS
IN FEDERAL REGULATION OF BUSINESS*

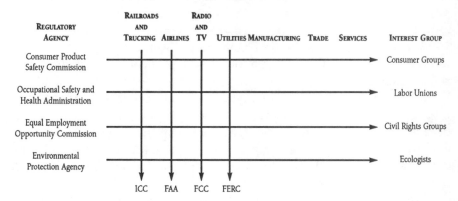

CATEGORY OF INDUSTRY OR SECTOR OF THE ECONOMY

*Source: Murray L. Weidenbaum, *Business, Government, and the Public*, 4th ed. (Englewood Cliffs, NJ: Prentice-Hall, 1990), p. 46, Figure 2.2.

The vertical lines in this figure show the traditional relationship between the old-style government commission or agency (ICC, Federal Aviation Administration [FAA], FCC) and the specific industry that it regulates. Most sectors of the economy—manufacturing, trade, and services—are virtually exempt from that type of intervention. In contrast, the horizontal lines show the newer social regulatory commissions and agencies (Environmental Protection Agency [EPA], Equal Employment Opportunity Commission [EEOC], Occupational Safety and Health Administration [OSHA], Consumer Product Safety Commission [CPSC]). The jurisdiction of these regulators extends to the great bulk of the private sector, cutting through whole segments of the marketplace.

Social regulation is not a new phenomenon. In fact, one of the first major pieces of federal regulatory legislation was the Animal and Plant Inspection Act of 1884. But compared to the past, the expansion of social regulation that has occurred in the United States since the 1960s has been massive.

Vogel has pointed out that prior to the 1960s, social regulatory programs were administered almost exclusively by state and local governments. From 1900 through 1965, only one regulatory agency was established at the federal level to protect either consumers, employees, or the public from physical harm due to business activities: the Food and Drug Administration, established in 1931. But between 1964 and 1977, 10 federal regulatory agencies were created in this area: the Equal Employment Opportunity Commission (1964), the National Transportation Safety Board (1966), the Council on Environmental Quality (1969), the Environmental Protection Agency (1970), the National Highway Traffic Safety Administration (1970), the Occupational Safety and Health Administration (1970), the Consumer Product Safety Commission (1972), the Mining Enforcement and Safety Administration (1973), the Materials Transportation Bureau (1975), and the Office of Strip Mining Regulation and Enforcement (1977).[7]

Vogel notes that in the broad area of consumer safety and health, only five laws were enacted by the federal government during the Progressive Era, eleven were enacted during the New Deal Era, but a total of 62 were enacted between 1964 and 1979. Only five pieces of national legislation dealt with job safety and other working conditions during the Progressive and New Deal eras, but between 1960 and 1978 21 new laws were enacted in this area. In the area of energy and environment, a total of seven

FIGURE 4.6
**THE INCREASING NUMBER OF
FEDERAL REGULATORY AGENCIES***

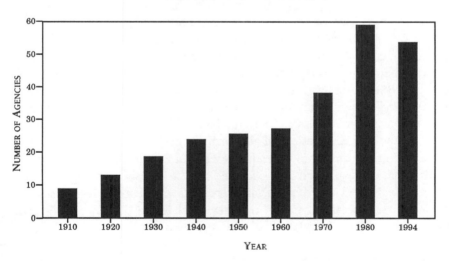

*Source: Murray L. Weidenbaum, *Business, Government, and the Public*, 4th ed. (Englewood Cliffs, NJ: Prentice-Hall, 1990), p. 21.

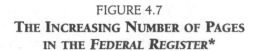

FIGURE 4.7
**THE INCREASING NUMBER OF PAGES
IN THE *FEDERAL REGISTER****

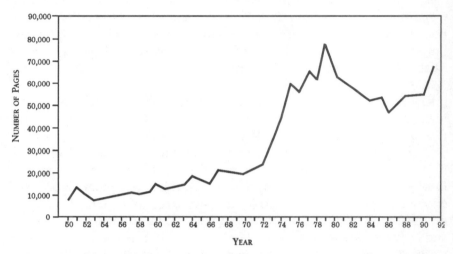

Source: Federal Register (Washington, DC: Office of the Federal Register, National Archives and Records Service, General Services Administration, various issues)

statutes were passed during the Progressive and New Deal eras, but no less than thirty-two were passed during the Social Regulation Era.[8]

Another illustration of the growth that has occurred in social regulation is the change in the number of regulatory agencies. Figure 4.6 shows the number of federal regulatory agencies from 1910 to 1990. As the figure clearly shows, more new agencies were added in the period from 1960 to 1979 than in any previous period. In fact, the number of regulatory agencies increased from 28 in the late 1950s to 59 by the late 1970s.

Yet another illustration of the growth in social regulations is the increase in the number of pages in the *Federal Register*. Figure 4.7 clearly shows that an explosion has occurred in the number of pages in the *Federal Register*. The *Federal Register* records proposed rules. A similar explosion has occurred in the number of pages in the *Code of Federal Regulations*, which records actual rules and regulations.

Costs of Regulation

No matter how we measure or document changes in the amount of federal regulation, the conclusion that a massive expansion occurred during the Social Regulation Era is inescapable. Could this expansion have influenced the NAIRU? To answer that question, we must have some idea about how much government regulation actually costs.

Thomas D. Hopkins of the Rochester Institute of Technology, a senior regulatory official in both the Reagan and Carter administrations, estimates that the total cost of complying with federal government regulations was about $581 billion (1991 dollars) in 1993.[9] This is more than $5,900 (1991 dollars) per U.S. household. We must note that Hopkins made no attempt to quantify benefits from federal regulatory efforts, and undoubtedly benefits do exist.

In order to understand Hopkins's estimates a little better, let us look at what Hopkins did and did not include in his estimates. Perhaps the first thing we should note is that Hopkins's study was designed to measure only nonbudgetary costs of federal regulation. In other words, the direct government budgetary expenditures of regulatory agencies are not included in Hopkins's estimates. The nonbudgetary costs of regulation can be divided into three general categories: compliance expenditures (what firms must spend to bring their operations into conformance with new regulation), productivity costs (the toll on innovation and cost control as a result of mandated expenditures), and consumer welfare reduction (higher consumer prices and limitations placed on consumer choices). In general, the Hopkins study includes only direct compliance costs. The other two categories are not included.

Hopkins divides the compliance costs into five specific categories. The first category is environmental regulation. Costs due to environmental regulations account for nearly one-quarter of Hopkins's estimated total regulatory costs in 1991. To obtain numbers on the compliance costs of environmental regulation, Hopkins relies on EPA estimates contained in a 1990 report. In this report, the EPA estimated annual compliance costs for all environmental regulations. Hopkins states that this report forms the heart of his analysis. Evidence exists that the EPA estimated costs are quite low when compared to actual costs. For instance, the EPA estimated that the cost to limit levels of radon in drinking water to 300 picocuries per liter would be $1.6 billion in capital costs and additional annual expenses of $180 million. But the Association of California Water Agencies found that the cost for meeting the radon standard in California alone would approach $3.7 billion. National costs were estimated at $12 to $20 billion, many times the EPA estimates.[10]

Hopkins's second category is other social regulation. Hopkins's estimates indicate that this category made up 7 percent of total regulatory costs in 1991. Other social regulation includes the host of programs that are intended to lessen risks to people in the workplace and as consumers. It includes regulation from agencies such as OSHA and the National Highway Traffic Safety Administration. To obtain estimates in this and the other remaining areas, Hopkins relies partly on estimates from previous research, specifically papers written by Robert W. Hahn and John A. Hird, Robert E. Litan and William D. Nordhaus, and Murray L. Weidenbaum and Robert DeFina,[11] and on estimates produced by various federal agencies.

A note of caution should be inserted here: federal agencies have an incentive to understate compliance costs. No agency wants to come under intense scrutiny or criticism for having imposed heavy costs on American businesses. Evidence abounds that agencies do, indeed, understate true compliance costs. We have already cited one example from the EPA. Another example involves the Department of Transportation. The National Research Council estimates that the Transportation Department's double-hull regulation relating to oil tankers will likely entail annual costs of more than $700 million, more than twice the amount estimated by the Transportation Department.[12] Yet another example involves the American Federation of Labor and Congress of Industrial Organizations (AFL-CIO). A Labor Department proposal to require union dues account changes has been criticized by the AFL-CIO as being excessively costly and for having understated cost estimates. The unions estimate costs at nearly $200 million, more than triple the government's estimate.[13]

The third category of regulation costs identified by Hopkins is economic regulation—efficiency costs. These are the costs associated with the loss of efficiency due to compliance with economic regulations. Hopkins estimates that in 1991, these costs accounted for 13 percent of the total, down from 23 percent in 1977, due to the deregulation efforts of the Carter and Reagan administrations.

The fourth category of costs, which Hopkins calls economic regulation—transfer costs, includes cost effects that penalize some so that others may gain. For instance, milk regulation redistributes about $500 million annually from consumers to producers. The Davis-Bacon Act and minimum wage laws transfer income from the rest of society to targeted workers. Hopkins estimates that such transfers accounted for 24 percent of total regulatory costs in 1991.

The final category of regulatory costs analyzed by Hopkins is referred to as process regulation. The major component of this category is paperwork and reporting obligations required by federal regulations. Hopkins's estimates come mainly from information on hours needed to comply with the paperwork and reporting requirements. He estimates that such costs accounted for 35 percent of all regulatory costs in 1991.

What conclusions can be reached regarding the Hopkins estimates? First, an exhaustive survey of the literature reveals that they are the most comprehensive estimates available. Hopkins should be commended for working in an area that few economists will even touch. Second, due to the extreme difficulty of measuring all of the costs of regulation,

TABLE 4.1
COSTS OF GOVERNMENT REGULATIONS
(BILLIONS OF DOLLARS)

Year	Administrative Costs	Growth of Adm. Costs (8%)	Hopkins's Total Regulatory Costs
1970	1.409		79
1971	1.731	22.9	97
1972	2.144	23.9	120
1973	2.727	27.2	153
1974	2.870	5.2	161
1975	3.438	19.8	193
1976	3.637	5.8	204
1977	4.276	17.6	240
1978	4.825	12.8	255
1979	5.558	15.2	281
1980	6.295	13.3	316
1981	6.555	4.1	343
1982	6.613	.9	354
1983	6.671	.9	358
1984	7.487	12.2	368
1985	7.944	6.1	376
1986	7.979	.4	377
1987	8.989	12.7	403
1988	9.931	10.5	410
1989	10.561	6.3	443
1990	11.563	9.5	490
1991	12.400	7.2	542
1992	13.591	9.6	581

Hopkins's estimates are undoubtedly incomplete and understated. As mentioned earlier, they do not include all of the productivity and welfare costs of federal regulation; they rely heavily on EPA estimates that may be suspect; and, of necessity, they rely on "guesstimates." Still, in spite of its incompleteness and its guesstimates, the Hopkins study reveals that the costs of federal regulation are huge.

But for our purpose of analyzing the effect of regulation on the U.S. NAIRU, we must be more concerned about *changes* in the costs of federal regulation. Have regulatory costs always been as huge as they are now? Unfortunately, the Hopkins' estimates go back only to the late 1970s, when the era of social regulation was reaching its peak. Hopkins does not provide estimates of regulatory costs before the Social Regulation Era began. The Center for the Study of American Business has provided numbers on the administrative costs of federal regulatory activities from 1970 to the present. We have used these numbers to estimate what the Hopkins estimates of federal government regulatory costs would have been from 1970 to 1977 had the costs of regulation grown at the same rate as federal administrative costs. Table 4.1 contains these estimates, together with Hopkins's estimated regulatory costs from 1977 to 1992.

Figure 4.8 shows the Hopkins estimates of regulatory costs, together with the projections going back to 1970. The figure clearly shows that regulatory costs increased strongly throughout the 1970s. The growth rate then leveled off during most of the 1980s but began to increase again beginning about 1988 and continuing through the first few years of the 1990s. In fact, Hopkins predicts that regulatory costs will increase significantly throughout the 1990s to the year 2000.

What was happening to the NAIRU in the 1970s, when regulatory costs were increasing? As already pointed out, the unemployment rate was also increasing. It, like regulatory costs, ceased its upward trend during the 1980s. If regulatory costs are now increasing again, might the NAIRU resume its upward trend? To help us answer this question, we need to gain a little perspective on how important regulatory costs are in our economy.

If Hopkins's estimates are in the ballpark, then regulatory costs now amount to about 10 percent of gross domestic product (GDP). In 1970, such costs accounted for, at most, 7 percent of GDP. And prior to the Social Regulatory Era, regulatory costs probably accounted for less than 5 percent of GDP, although this is only a guesstimate. According to Hopkins's estimates, regulatory costs equal 20 percent of all of the wages

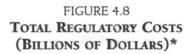

FIGURE 4.8
**TOTAL REGULATORY COSTS
(BILLIONS OF DOLLARS)***

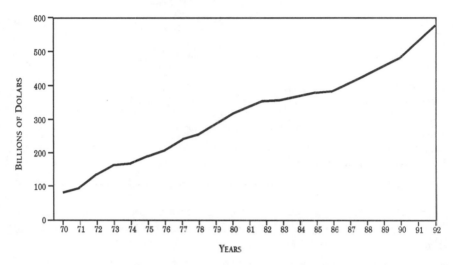

*Source: Thomas D. Hopkins, "The Costs of Federal Regulation," *Policy Analysis* (Washington, DC: National Chamber Foundation, 1992); Thomas D. Hopkins, "Costs of Regulation," report prepared for the Regulatory Information Service Center, August 1992; and Melinda Warren, *Mixed Message: An Analysis of the 1994 Federal Regulatory Budget*, Occasional Paper 128 (St. Louis, Missouri: Center for the Study of American Business, August 1993), Table A-4.

and salaries paid to employees in the United States. Clearly, regulatory costs cannot be ignored in explaining why unemployment has increased in the United States. We cannot ignore the current upward trend in these costs, if we are to reduce the unemployment rate.

Paul W. MacAvoy has provided another estimate of the costs of government regulation.[14] He has estimated the average annual percentage increases in operating and capital costs associated with regulatory compliance during the 1973-81 and 1981-87 periods for several industries that he argues were the most affected by increasing social regulations. Table 4.2 contains his estimates. The estimates are average annual percentage changes due to regulatory costs, including return to capital equipment required by the EPA, OSHA, and the National Health, Transportation, and Safety Admininstration (NHTSA) and the average of

TABLE 4.2
**MacAvoy's Estimates of Cost Increases
Due to Regulatory Compliance**

Industry	1973-81	1981-87
Metal and coal mining	5.8	0.0
Stone, glass, and clay and primary metalindustries	2.9	0.1
Motor vehicles	5.6	3.5
Nondurable manufacturing	4.2	0.9

operating costs for EPA and NHTSA regulations. In other words, the estimates understate the costs of regulation since the costs associated with
the regulations of many federal agencies are not included.

The table shows that current-year recovery of the described costs during the 1973-81 period would have justified price increases of 5 to 6 percent per annum in the mining and automobile industries, 4 percent per
annum in nondurable manufacturing, and 3 percent per annum in construction products and primary metals. If MacAvoy's estimates are correct, there can be little doubt that increased costs associated with the
Social Regulation Era contributed significantly to inflation during the
1973-81 period and thus to an increasing NAIRU. MacAvoy's estimates,
like those of Hopkins, show that regulatory cost increases moderated during the 1980s. This corresponds to a period when the NAIRU was not
increasing.

Several studies have employed a general equilibrium framework to
analyze the effects of regulation on the economy. For instance, Dale
Jorgenson and Peter Wilcoxen have argued that environmental regulation
alone reduced GDP by 2.6 percent annually over the 1975-83 period.[15]
Michael Hazilla and Raymond Kopp, also using a general equilibrium
approach, come up with even higher estimated effects. They argue that
real GNP was 5.8 percent lower in 1990 than it would have been without
clean air and clear water regulations.[16]

Could the massive buildup of regulatory costs just described have
contributed to an increase in the NAIRU? The answer is clearly yes.
Economic theory predicts that substantial increases in the costs of doing

business lead to more unemployment. In real terms, the costs of regulation have undoubtedly increased greatly. Regulatory costs are not the sole factor contributing to the increasing U.S. unemployment rate (we discuss several others in the coming chapters), but the importance of regulatory costs cannot be ignored.

State and Local Government Regulation

Before leaving this subject, note should be made that the foregoing discussion referred only to federal regulation. State and local governments also are heavily involved in regulation. In fact, as the federal government eased some regulations under President Reagan, the states started tightening their grip on business. Samuel Brunelli, president of the American Legislative Exchange Council, has stated that "states are flexing their muscles, and they're becoming much tougher and more burdensome in regulations than even the feds on these issues."[17]

In another paper, Bruce A. Williams has stated that while most popular and scholarly attention has focused on the federal government's activities, states were actively involved in regulating market relations, often in minute detail, long before the federal government became involved. He points out that as the American economy became national in scope, the federal government became an increasingly important source of regulatory authority. As it rose to prominence, however, it tended to supplement—rather than supplant—the states' regulatory efforts.[18]

Williams notes that according to political scientist Emmette S. Redford, the regulatory powers possessed by the states can be divided into four different areas:

> 1. Areas of authority mandated to the states by the constitution or left to the states as a result of congressional inaction. States, for example, maintain the jurisdiction to define the rights of property owners, as well as the jurisdiction to limit those rights and to regulate the ways in which property can be transmitted. States also regulate employer-employee relationships through the workers' compensation system, laws governing the ability of unions to establish closed shops, and laws relating to such issues as the minimum number of workers necessary for any particular project, and so on. They regulate the provision of some collective goods, such as public services like road construction and maintenance, school construction and staffing, and recreational facilities. States have always regulated labor relations and the activities of

businesses, trades, and professions that are intrastate in nature.

2. Regulatory authority delegated to states by the federal government. Included here are areas of policy that, while falling under federal authority, have been specifically delegated back to the states by Congress; a variety of regulatory activities are of this type. Insurance regulation was returned to the states under the McCarran-Furgeson Act, after the federal courts ruled that the insurance industry was involved in interstate commerce. The licensing and rate regulation of hydroelectric projects is controlled by the state, unless the state chooses not to create a commission for this purpose. Price maintenance agreements authorized by states have been exempted from federal antitrust statutes. Similarly, states may exercise jurisdiction in labor disputes when the National Labor Relations Board does not assert its authority. Where a state commission for the regulation of public utilities' security exists, the federal government stands aside. Moreover, in several regulatory acts of Congress (e.g. the Occupational Safety and Health Act), the states may opt to enforce the provision themselves.

3. Areas of parallel activity where both the states and the federal government exercise authority. Both levels of government maintain regulatory agencies that oversee utility rate levels and structures, banking practices, securities transactions, railroad rates and services, labor relations, and some areas of consumer protection.

4. Areas of cooperation between the states and the federal government. Most congressional regulatory legislation attempts to establish cooperative relationships between state and federal agencies, even when the federal government is the source of regulatory legislation; in such cases, federal regulators are usually highly dependent on the activities of state-level officials. Provisions for such cooperation are found in regulations affecting environmental protection, some areas of consumer protection, occupational safety and health, communications, power, natural gas, and motor carriers, among others.

States are obviously involved in a great deal of regulatory activity. In fact, the preceeding information seems to indicate that state government regulation may be as important and costly as federal government regulation. If this is, indeed, the case, then total state government regulation may cost as much as $500 billion annually and the grand total of all government regulation, including costs due to state and local regulations as well as federal regulations, may be well over $1,000 billion.

CONCLUSIONS AND RECOMMENDATIONS

If government regulations at the federal level, as well as state and local levels, add significantly to business costs and increase the NAIRU, then what steps should we take? The most important step is to educate legislators, other government officials, and the public about the costs of regulations and the impact regulations have on unemployment. We often hear talk about the need for legislators and regulators to conduct cost-benefit analyses of proposed regulations before they are enacted. The federal government has actually made attempts to require regulators to produce such analyses. President Gerald Ford issued an executive order creating an Inflation Impact Statement program in November 1974. It required that major federal proposals for legislation, rules, and regulations be accompanied by a statement analyzing their inflationary impact. The name of the program was later changed to the Economic Impact Statement program to reflect a broader emphasis on assessing the impact of legislation, rules, and regulations on market costs, productivity, competition, and supplies of important products.[19] President Ford's program, while well intentioned, was limited in its scope and impact. Too many agencies and types of regulations were exempted and few statements were ever actually filed.

Further attempts at requiring analysis of the costs of regulations have occurred during the past 15 years. In 1981, Executive Order 12291 was issued. It directed regulators to produce a Regulatory Impact Analysis containing cost information for every major new regulation. Executive Order 12498, issued in 1985, directed regulators annually to provide the Office of Management and Budget (OMB) with information about all of their new, significant regulatory actions. Bulletin No. 91-04, issued by the OMB in 1990, lets regulators know that the information required to be provided to the OMB should include cost estimates, among other things, and this bulletin explains how these estimates are to be presented. In addition, both Executive Order 12291 and the Regulatory Flexibility Act require that the Regulatory Information Service Center gather summary information semiannually about virtually every new federal regulatory activity and encourage regulators to include cost estimates.[20]

According to Hopkins, in practice, the requisite analyses and cost estimates are not always produced, and even when they are produced, no easy and systematic way exists to cumulate their costs to attain an estimate of the overall cost burden of regulation. Our work emphasizes the importance of such analyses. Regulations have real and very important impacts on inflation and unemployment. We do not doubt that many regulations have benefits, but how often are those benefits weighed against the costs of unemployment? Government requirements concerning cost estimates should be strengthened.

In January 1993, Senator Orrin Hatch introduced legislation that would accomplish this purpose. The first two sections of this legislation follow:

SECTION 1. SHORT TITLE.
This Act may be cited as the "Regulatory Accountability Act of 1993."

SECTION 2. CONGRESSIONAL FINDINGS AND STATEMENT OF PURPOSE.
a. FINDINGS.—The Congress finds and declares that—
(1) the overall cost of Federal regulation in the United States has risen to well over $400,000,000,000 per year;
(2) this regulatory burden is paid by individual citizens and their families in the form of a "hidden tax" because intermediaries have no options that do not pass these expenditures to individuals;
(3) the most recent data reveals that the "hidden tax" paid by citizens of the Nation now exceeds $4,100 annually for each household;
(4) left unchecked, this "hidden tax" will increase by 50 percent between now and the year 2000; and
(5) it is in the best interests of the American people to have the Federal Government devise a systematic way to account for the new regulatory costs that taxpayers are forced to absorb and to have this financial burden better controlled.

b. PURPOSE.—It is the purpose of this Act to establish that each agency shall, as a mandatory requirement for the issuance of—
(1) any proposed regulation—
    (A) thoroughly assess and document the anticipated benefits, reasonable alternative approaches, and all foreseeable compliance costs of each approach; and
    (B) assess, and include in all proposed regulatory actions, a range of possible offsets for the costs; and
(2) any final regulation—
    (A) have selected the most cost-effective alternative; and
    (B) for a period of 3 years following enactment, have fully offset all foreseeable costs through revocation or revision of one or more existing regulations.

This act would require agencies to assess the costs of their proposed regulations before they are enacted and offset those costs with revocations or revisions of existing regulations. If we are to reduce the unemployment rate that is consistent with stable inflation, the inflation and unemployment costs of government regulations must be well known, actively debated, and considered before legislation is passed and regulations enacted. This book recommends that the currently languishing Regulatory Accountability Act of 1993, which has apparently been stuck in a congressional committee, be quickly enacted. The benefit to our society is a focusing of attention on the employment and inflationary impacts of social regulations.

NOTES

1. Edmund S. Phelps, *Structural Slumps: The Modern Equilibrium Theory of Unemployment, Interest, and Assets* (Cambridge: Harvard University Press, 1994).

2. Richard Layard, *How to Beat Unemployment* (Oxford, England: Oxford University Press, 1986), p. 38.

3. David Vogel, "The 'New' Social Regulation in Historical and Comparative Perspective," in Thomas K. McCraw (ed.), *Regulation in Perspective* (Cambridge: Harvard University Press, 1981), pp. 155-86.

4. Larry N. Gerston, Cynthia Fraleigh, and Robert Schwab, *The Deregulated Society* (Pacific Grove, CA: Brooks/Cole, 1988), pp. 24-25.

5. Ibid., p. 27.

6. Murray L. Weidenbaum, *Business, Government, and the Public*, 4th ed. (Englewood Cliffs, NJ: Prentice-Hall, 1990), p. 46, Figure 2.2.

7. Vogel, "The 'New' Social Regulation," p. 161.

8. Ibid., p. 162.

9. Thomas D. Hopkins, "The Costs of Federal Regulation," *Policy Analysis* (Washington, DC: National Chamber Foundation, 1992); Thomas D. Hopkins, "Costs of Regulation: Filling the Gaps," report prepared for the Regulatory Information Service Center, August 1992; "Cost of Regulation Isn't Easy to Figure but Estimates Exist," *Wall Street Journal*, September 23, 1992, p. A6.

10. *Science*, January 8, 1993, p. 159.

11. Robert W. Hahn and John A. Hird, "The Costs and Benefits of Regulation: Review and Synthesis," *Yale Journal on Regulation* 8 (Winter 1991), pp. 233-78; Robert E. Litan and William D. Nordhaus, *Reforming Federal Regulation* (New Haven, CT: Yale University Press, 1983); and Murray L. Weidenbaum and

Robert DeFina, *The Cost of Federal Regulation of Economic Activity* (Washington, DC: American Enterprise Institute, May 1978).

12. National Research Council, *Tanker Spills: Prevention by Design* (Washington, DC: National Academy Press, 1991).

13. *Wall Street Journal*, June 23, 1992, p. A1.

14. Paul W. MacAvoy, *Industry Regulation and the Performance of the American Economy* (New York: Norton, 1992).

15. Dale W. Jorgenson and Peter J. Wilcoxen, "Environmental Regulation and U.S. Economic Growth," *Rand Journal of Economics* 21 (Summer 1990), p. 315.

16. Michael Hazilla and Raymond J. Kopp, "Social Cost of Environmental Quality Regulations: A General Equilibrium Analysis," *Journal of Political Economy* 98 (August 1990), pp. 853-73.

17. David Warner, "Watch the States," *Nation's Business*, November 1990, pp. 15-23.

18. Bruce A. Williams, "Bounding Behavior: Economic Regulation in the American States," in Virginia Gray, Herbert Jacob, and Kenneth N. Vines (eds.), *Politics in the American States: A Comparative Analysis*, 4th ed. (Boston: Little, Brown, 1983), pp. 329-372.

19. Charles W. Vernon III, "The Inflation Impact Statement Program: An Assessment of the First Two Years," *American University Law Review* 26 (Summer 1977), pp. 1138-68.

20. Hopkins, "The Costs of Federal Regulation."

CHAPTER 5

UNEMPLOYMENT INSURANCE, SOCIAL WELFARE, AND THE NAIRU

The headline of a May 1993 article on the editorial page of the *Wall Street Journal* proclaimed, "To Ensure Unemployment, Insure It."[1] In other words, all we have to do to ensure that the United States has a great deal of unemployed workers is to pay people to be unemployed. The article specifically argued that extending the time period during which people can receive unemployment insurance benefits may increase the unemployment rate. Does unemployment insurance increase unemployment in general and the NAIRU in particular?

This chapter analyzes the U.S. unemployment insurance system and asks whether it has contributed to an increase in the NAIRU. It also briefly examines the broader topic of the effect of social welfare payments in general on unemployment. Let us begin with a brief review of the history of unemployment insurance in the United States and an outline of the essential elements of our present system. Then let us roughly examine the relationship between unemployment insurance coverage and actual unemployment.

UNEMPLOYMENT INSURANCE IN THE UNITED STATES

The U.S. unemployment insurance (UI) program was enacted as part of the Social Security Act in 1935. It was intended to be a self-financing social insurance program that levied payroll taxes on covered employers and paid benefits to eligible unemployed workers. Currently, workers laid off by their employers are potentially eligible to collect benefits for a limited time, usually 26 weeks, until they are recalled, find another job exhaust their benefits, or leave the labor force. Most unemployed workers now receive a maximum of between 50 and 60 percent of their previous wages, depending on which state they live in.

UI in the United States is a hybrid federal-state system in which responsibilities are shared between these two levels of government. This sharing of responsibility is a central component of the UI program. In fact, according to some analysts, in no other public program have responsibilities been so thoroughly shared between the federal and state governments.[2]

The federal-state nature of the system was dictated by circumstances in 1935. Not enough was known then about the impact of the many ingredients of unemployment insurance to warrant imposing untried provisions on an entire nation. Moreover, there was doubt that such a system could even be enacted by a state-oriented Congress. Finally, President Roosevelt favored a cooperative federal-state undertaking.

The real issue in 1935 was not whether there would or would not be a sharing of responsibilities but rather the best possible division of responsibilities. The system could have been structured so as to render states little more than the federal government's administrative agents, at one extreme, or so as to give the states near total autonomy, at the other. The decision, expressed by President Roosevelt's Committee on Economic Security and later by Congress in enacting the Social Security Act, was to give states as much autonomy as possible, consistent with prescribed national objectives:

> The plan for unemployment compensation that we suggest contemplates that the states shall have broad freedom to set up the type of unemployment compensation they wish. We believe that all matters in which uniformity is not absolutely essential should be left to the States.[3]

Accordingly, under the U.S. UI system, states alone determine what minimum wage or employment requirements must be satisfied by any individual to qualify for benefits. The states decide the formulas used to determine individual weekly benefit amounts, minimum and maximum benefit levels, the payment of partial benefits, and the availability and amount of dependents' allowances. The states have almost complete authority in establishing the availability-for-work, ability-to-work, and work search requirements individuals must meet to maintain their eligibility for benefits. In addition, the states are basically free to establish the causes for disqualification from benefits and the particular disqualification penalty, and they have wide discretion over how liability for taxes will be allocated among employers, and total authority to determine the amount of taxes to be collected.

What about the federal government? The Committee on Economic Security identified four key *federal* responsibilities: (1) providing an incentive for states to act; (2) safeguarding unemployment reserves; (3) ensuring efficient administration; and (4) providing program standards where uniformity was essential.

The immediate federal responsibility in 1935 was to provide an incentive for states to enact and maintain unemployment insurance laws. Thus, the Social Security Act provided businesses with a competitive disadvantage if their state did not become part of the UI program. It established a federal unemployment tax (originally 3 percent, currently 6.2 percent) and allowed credit against the tax to employers who pay taxes under a state law that meets federal requirements. Thus, the federal law allows states to void most of the 6.2 percent federal tax. The states are then free to construct sets of schedules that vary the tax rate charged to individual plants so long as overall financial solvency is maintained.

The tax credit provision embodies a compelling incentive for a state to adopt not only an unemployment insurance program but also minimum coverage and taxable wage base standards. For all potentially eligible employers to actually receive credit against the 6.2 percent federal tax, the same employers, employment, and wages that are subject to the federal tax must also be subject to state law. A state that excluded the construction trades or banking industry, for example, would deprive those employers of the opportunity to receive credit against the federal tax.

The tax credit approach also embodies the principal penalty for failure of a state to enact an unemployment insurance law or to conform with a multitude of federal requirements. The denial of tax credit is so formidable a penalty that no state is willing to risk the hazard.

The national interest in making coverage almost universal was accomplished by gradually eliminating exclusions from the federal tax. In 1935, the tax applied to employers with eight or more workers. The tax was extended to employers with four or more in 1950, and the present one or more in 1970. Large farm employers and some domestic service employers were covered by 1976 legislation limiting the previous exclusions. In 1970 and 1976, coverage was extended to nonprofit organizations employing four or more and to most state and local government workers.

The Social Security Act provides for the establishment of an Unemployment Trust Fund in the U.S. Treasury. It authorizes the secretary of the treasury to invest amounts in the fund not needed to meet current withdrawals. A separate bookkeeping account is maintained for each state UI agency, and the secretary is required to pay out of the fund to any state agency whatever amount it requisitions from its account. Both the Social Security Act and the Federal Unemployment Tax Act require that each state immediately deposit all contributions collected under the state UI law into the Unemployment Trust Fund—and that moneys withdrawn from that fund be used only for unemployment compensation.

Eight-tenths of 1 percent of the state unemployment tax that is paid to the federal government is kept by the federal government. The federal government uses this money for two things. First, the revenues are used to finance the administrative costs of the states' UI claims operations and their employment service functions. Second, the revenues are used to establish a pool of funds from which advances can be given to states that have depleted their funds for benefits.

The 1935 Social Security Act also included the following labor standards requirement:

> Compensation shall not be denied in such State to any otherwise eligible individual for refusing to accept new work under any of the following conditions: (A) if the position offered is vacant due directly to a strike, lockout, or other labor dispute; (B) if the wages, hours, or other conditions of work are substantially less favorable to the individual than those prevailing for similar work in the locality; (C) if as a condition of being employed the individual would be required to join a company union or refrain from joining any bona fide labor organization.

In 1970, federal law was amended to require that all states participate in a plan that combines the wages and employment of an individual who worked in more than one state so that eligibility for, and the amount of, benefits could be based on the combined wages and work when applying the provisions of a single state.

The most significant *federal* standard enacted since 1935 was the establishment in 1970 of a permanent standby program of extended benefits. It requires states to provide additional levels of benefits during heavy periods of unemployment for individuals who have exhausted their regular entitlement. The program is financed on a 50-50 federal-state basis. Up to 13 extra weeks of benefits are permitted at the claimant's usual weekly benefit amount. These extended benefits are triggered if the state's insured unemployment rate (IUR) for the past 13-week period is 20 percent higher than the rate for the corresponding period in the past two years and the rate is at least 5 percent. The 20 percent requirement can be waived if state law so permits, provided the rate is at least 6 percent. Extended benefits cease to become available when the IUR does not meet either the 20 percent requirement or the 5 or 6 percent requirement, whichever is applicable. States have no choice other than to enact the extended benefits program totally. They have no discretion over the terms and conditions under which extended benefits are paid.

During the 1980s, the federal government curtailed the permanent extended benefits program somewhat. First, a national trigger, which provided that when nationwide unemployment rates reached prescribed levels, extended benefits would become available to all states, was eliminated. Second, the level of insured unemployment necessary to activate the state trigger was increased. Prior to passage of the amendment, extended benefits became payable when a state's IUR averaged 4 percent or more for 13 weeks and was at least 120 percent of average IUR for the corresponding 13-week period in the preceding two years. A state could opt to disregard the 120 percent requirement and trigger the extended benefits if its current 13-week rate was as much as 5 percent. The 1981 amendment increased from 4 to 5 percent the required state IUR trigger level and from 5 to 6 percent the optional trigger level for states choosing to waive the 120 percent requirement. Third, the method of calculating the IUR was changed. Prior to the change, the IUR calculation included individuals filing claims for extended benefits as well as regular benefit claimants. The amendment eliminated extended benefits claimants from the count.

Another change in UI that occurred in the 1980s has to do with taxation of UI benefits. In 1979, President Carter signed a law requiring recipients of unemployment benefits to pay taxes on those benefits if their income was above a certain threshold. In 1982, President Reagan reduced the threshold. In 1986, the Tax Reform Act reduced the threshold to zero. Thus, the tax laws of the 1980s reduced the size of unemployment benefits relative to wages, making work relatively more attractive.

UI AND THE INCREASE IN UNEMPLOYMENT

We have shown that the NAIRU rate has increased significantly between 1960 and the present. We have also pointed out that the U.S. unemployment insurance program was enacted considerably before the 1960s, in 1935. In order for the argument that unemployment insurance

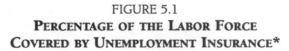

FIGURE 5.1
**PERCENTAGE OF THE LABOR FORCE
COVERED BY UNEMPLOYMENT INSURANCE***

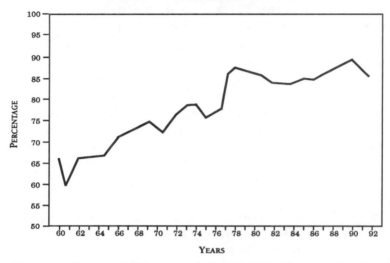

*Source: *Statistical Abstract of the United States 1993*, 113th ed. (Washington, DC: U.S. Department of Commerce, Economics and Statistics Administration, Bureau of the Census, 1993.

contributed to an increasing unemployment rate in the period from 1960 to 1990 to be valid, it must be demonstrated that significant changes occurred in the program during this period. As just outlined, significant changes did occur. The unemployment insurance tax was extended to employers with only one employee in 1970 and extended to farm employers, nonprofit organizations, and state and local governments in the 1970s. Richard Vedder and Lowell Gallaway have pointed out that during the period from 1961 to 1969, two-thirds of the U.S. civilian labor force was in employment covered by the UI program. By the 1974-79 period, more than 80 percent was in covered employment.[4] Figure 5.1 shows the percentage of the civilian labor force in employment covered by unemployment compensation over the 1960 to 1991 period.

In spite of these changes making unemployment insurance coverage more broad, other changes in the program appear to have had the effect of making the program less generous. Unemployment insurance benefits began to be taxed in the 1980s, and the UI extended benefits program was made less generous. In addition, fiscally strapped states also introduced tighter eligibility controls in the 1980s. In fact, the percentage of the unemployed receiving UI was only 39 percent during the 1991-92 recession, down from 43 percent in 1980 and around 50 percent in the 1960s and 1970s.

What conclusions can be reached? The proportion of workers covered by UI expanded during the 1970s, perhaps contributing to an increase in the NAIRU. However, tighter eligibility requirements and other changes in UI in the 1980s should have made work relatively more attractive, and yet the unemployment rate has apparently not receded. From this evidence, the argument can be made that changes in the UI program played, at most, only a minor role in the United States' increasing NAIRU.

OTHER SOCIAL WELFARE PROGRAMS

Unemployment insurance is not, by any means, the only social welfare program that can potentially affect unemployment. Any program that cushions the economic effects of unemployment may increase unemployment. Let us be clear. This does not, in any way, mean that all such programs are bad. It simply means that, through their effect on work incentives they have the *potential* to raise the level of unemployment.

Many social welfare programs have been enacted or expanded since 1960. The food stamp, Medicaid, Medicare, Supplemental Security Income, and other new programs have all been put in place since 1960. President Lyndon B. Johnson's "War on Poverty" began after 1960. In general, funding for social welfare programs has increased dramatically since 1960. Figure 5.2 shows that social welfare expenditures by all governments in the United States increased from about 13 percent of personal income in 1960 to about 22 percent by the end of the 1970s. Even after subtracting education and Social Security expenditures from the total, social welfare expenditures still doubled as a percentage of personal income between 1960 and 1980 and stabilized at that higher level through the 1980s. Let us recall that it was also during the 1960s and 1970s that the U.S. unemployment rate increased, and it, too, stabilized at its higher level through the 1980s. As pointed out by Vedder and Gallaway, such a growth in the relative importance of the "safety net" alters people's attitudes about what is an acceptable job and an acceptable wage rate.[5] It increases the real wage demanded by workers without a corresponding increase in productivity and thus increases the NAIRU.

FIGURE 5.2
U.S. SOCIAL EXPENDITURES AS A PERCENTAGE OF PERSONAL INCOME*

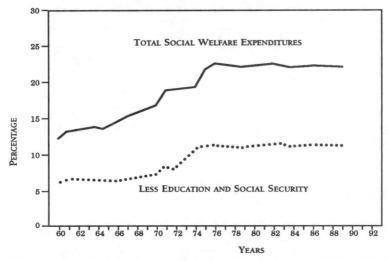

*Source: *Statistical Abstract of the United States 1993*, 113th ed. (Washington, DC: U.S. Department of Commerce, Economics and Statistics Administration, Bureau of the Census, 1993.

EUROPE'S EXPERIENCE

Europe has extended the safety net much further than has the United States. What can be learned from its experience? Let's look first at the unemployment insurance systems of Europe. The typical European UI system differs from that of the United States in at least two important respects. First, the replacement ratio (the ratio of unemployment benefits to previous income) is typically higher in most European countries. David R. Henderson points out that a single 40-year-old worker previously employed at the 1988 production worker wage could get unemployment benefits equal to 59 percent of previous earnings in France, 58 percent in Germany, and 70 percent in the Netherlands. This compares to about 50 percent for U.S. workers.[6]

Gary Burtless, an economist whose work is discussed by Henderson, has noted that the difference between the U.S. replacement ratio and that of the typical European country is higher than the simple difference between the two seems to indicate. The typical European worker is covered by government-provided health insurance, whereas the typical

American worker gets health insurance through his or her employer. Therefore, when a U.S. worker loses his or her job, he or she gets UI benefits worth about 50 percent of the previous wage, not 50 percent of the previous total compensation that included health insurance. When a European worker loses his or her job, he or she not only receives a check for, on average, 60 percent of the previous wage but also keeps the government-provided health insurance, which increases significantly the replacement ratio.[7]

The second difference between U.S. unemployment insurance and that found in the typical European country is the length of time unemployed workers can receive benefits. We have already noted that UI usually lasts for only 26 weeks in the United States. In France, the maximum duration is two and a half years. In Germany, there are a maximum of one year for unemployment insurance and no maximum for unemployment assistance, the benefits of which are almost as high as unemployment insurance. In the Netherlands, the maximum duration is three years.

What about European social welfare payments in general? We have noted that in the United States, government social welfare expenditures now amount to about 23 percent of personal income or 15 percent of GDP. In Europe, the typical government spends at least 25 percent of its GDP on social welfare. The safety net is indeed much stronger and broader in Europe.

What have been the unemployment results of Europe's extensive safety net provisions? Some have argued that more unemployment has been the result. During the 1982-92 decade, unemployment in the European Community averaged close to 10 percent; even during peaks in business activity, the unemployment rate did not fall below 9 percent. In contrast, the U.S. unemployment rate averaged 6.8 percent over the same decade, reaching a low of 5.3 percent in 1989 and never topping 7.5 percent. In addition, much of Europe's unemployment has been long-term in nature. In 1989, only 1.2 percent of the U.S. labor force was unemployed for longer than 13 weeks. Corresponding rates for most European countries were four to seven times as high. For even longer-term unemployment, the numbers are worse. Whereas only 0.3 percent of people in the U.S. labor force were unemployed for one year or more, the European countries had rates of 3.0 to 5.6 percent. Only 6 percent of all unemployed people in the United States were counted as unemployed for 12 or more months. In Europe the corresponding numbers ranged from 49 percent in Germany to 72 percent in Italy.[8]

In a 1994 discussion of the industrialized countries' unemployment problems, the International Monetary Fund had this to say of Europe and the United States:

> Compared with those in Europe, labor markets in the United States are more flexible—reflecting, among other things, less generous unemployment insurance provisions in terms of the level of benefit payments, duration of benefits, and qualification for benefits; wider earnings dispersions; lower levels of unionization and less centralized wage bargaining; less government intervention in the wage bargaining process; fewer restrictions on hiring or firing of employees; and lower social insurance charges and other nonwage labor costs, such as the amount of paid vacation.[9]

Europe's experiments with unemployment insurance and social welfare seem to show that the more unemployment is subsidized, the more people will choose to be unemployed and will remain so for longer periods of time. In fact, Lawrence Katz and Bruce Meyer have shown that even a modest extension of unemployment benefits can have significant effects on unemployment. These economists examined what effect a 13-week extension of benefits had on the duration of unemployment. They found that it increased the average duration of unemployment for someone receiving unemployment benefits by 2.2 weeks, from 16.2 weeks to 18.4 weeks.[10] This seemingly small increase translates into a significant increase in the overall unemployment rate.

The evidence seems to indicate that the U.S. unemployment insurance system has probably not contributed significantly to unemployment. The U.S. social welfare system, in general, may have. Under the Clinton administration, the United States has shown signs of moving closer to the European style of social welfare system. The administration greatly admires parts of Germany's system and would like to extend the so-called safety net farther than it is now extended. In terms of unemployment, such a move would definitely be in the wrong direction. It would likely cause unemployment to increase and thereby result in a net decrease in social welfare, not an increase.

One European country, however, has had an unemployment record that is virtually unmatched in the industrialized world—Sweden. During the 1980s, when most of Europe had unemployment rates close to 10 percent, Sweden's rate averaged about 2.1 percent and it never topped 3 percent. Such evidence invites an examination of Sweden's unemployment insurance system and philosophy.

SWEDEN'S APPROACH: THE "EMPLOYMENT STRATEGY"

Sweden's philosophy regarding unemployment is what some have called the employment strategy.[11] This philosophy stands in contrast to the so-called cash assistance strategy used by most other countries. The employment strategy means that if a person wants an income, he or she should have the opportunity to earn it rather than depend on cash transfers from others. If people do not have work, the key objective is to improve their employability. The Swedish philosophy is that no one should be allowed to sink into passive inactivity.

According to Richard Layard and John Philpott, from this basic philosophy, two things follow. First, indefinite receipt of benefits is ruled out. Benefits in Sweden are generous, but they last only 14 months. This limitation on indefinite benefits is similar to the U.S. approach but stands in contrast to the approach taken by many other European countries. Second, an active labor market policy ensures that long before unemployment benefits run out, most of the unemployed have been placed in work, after training, if necessary. In Sweden, those who aren't working after the 14 months become legally entitled to a temporary 6-month public sector job, at normal rates of pay. The Swedish program is designed to preserve people's employability and self-respect. Let's consider the nuts and bolts of how the Swedes accomplish this goal.

About 80 percent of all Swedish workers are entitled to unemployment insurance if they are unemployed. To be so entitled, workers must be a member of the unemployment fund associated with their occupation for at least a year. In order to draw benefits an individual must also work at least 75 days within the previous 12 months.

Since not everybody is a member of a UI fund, a parallel system of support operates for other workers, including people with no work record. This alternative system is called cash assistance (KAS), and people can qualify by staying in school to age 17 as well as by work. But nobody under 20 can draw KAS. KAS generally lasts only 150 days (seven months).

The level of UI in Sweden is one of the most generous in the world, but it is subject to a relatively severe work test. A worker on UI gets 90 percent of his former wage. The cash assistance program is much less generous.[12]

When someone becomes unemployed, he or she goes to a job center, not to an unemployment benefit office. The receptionist there supplies the forms to apply for UI/KAS. The person must fill in a daily record of his or her unemployment and send it to the UI/KAS administration about once every two weeks. The person receives his or her first benefit check after about three weeks.

The Swedish work test functions as follows. The employment office provides the worker regularly with lists of vacancies he or she should pursue. If a job offer comes along, it must be accepted if it pays the standard rate for the job, if it is within the bounds of existing job opportunities, and if adequate consideration has been given to the person's background and suitability for the work, as well as personal aspects of the job. Workers can be expected to take different jobs from their previous job from the moment they register, and, if necessary, they are expected to leave an area of high unemployment for one where there are more jobs. But they are not expected to take jobs paying less than 90 percent of their benefit entitlement.

If a worker refuses a suitable job or training, he or she loses UI benefits for four weeks. The employment office simply refers the case to the managers of the relevant insurance fund (or the board that runs the KAS). In the vast majority of cases the authorities accept the reference and stop paying the benefit. The individual can appeal but is generally unsuccessful. If a person refuses work three times, he or she can be permanently disqualified until he or she has clearly reestablished a work record. This work test is not an idle tool. It is used and is taken quite seriously.

The whole labor market policy pivots around the placement and counseling system, which costs about 0.18 percent of Sweden's GNP. According to Layard and Philpott, the quality of the system is remarkable.[13]

At the job centers, each registering unemployed person is interviewed by a senior placement officer—or a counselor if more general advice is wanted (including such issues as further education). At this interview, the person agrees with the officer on a job search strategy and how frequently the person will report to the office (usually at least once a month). For these subsequent interviews, the person is allocated a personal placement officer, to whom he or she remains attached until a job is found. The employment service is also available to workers who already have jobs. About half of those who are placed are not unemployed. This may mean that workers can move from underemployed situations to more fully employed situations, and the efficiency of the economy may increase as a result.

The placement officer's key tool is his computer terminal. On it, he or she has a detailed record of every registered vacancy in Sweden (about

60-70 percent of all vacancies are registered). This vacancies database is continually updated. The placement officer not only has a caseload of job seekers but also has a caseload of firms. He or she must understand their requirements and enter their vacancies into the national bank of vacancies.

Assume a worker wants a job as a plumber in Stockholm. The officer can at once print out details of all such jobs. Commonly, the placement officer will send a client a computer printout of suitable vacancies each week. According to Layard and Philpott, it is now possible in many offices for unemployed people to have direct access to a terminal at any time.[14]

The employment service is designed to be a service to employers as well as to workers. For this purpose, the computer also has a complete register of all the unemployed in the country—their skills and their desires. Thus, if a firm in Stockholm wants a plumber, it can be given a printout with details of workers looking for such a job.

The computer system is thus a virtual labor market, not much different from the computer system through which many stock exchanges operate. In both situations, it is difficult and costly to match demands and supplies, albeit with a high-quality computer system can it be done with great efficiency. In effect, such a system can reduce the frictional part of unemployment.

If the placement office is not able to place an unemployed worker in a new job, he or she still has the training or retraining option. In fact, this option is considered from the outset. If the individual's skill level is clearly antiquated, he or she needs to retrain—and some may actually embark on training even before becoming redundant and perhaps thereby prevent some unemployment. The average person entering training has been unemployed for three to five months.

Placement officers have an additional option that becomes available after six months of unemployment. They can offer firms a financial inducement (of 50 percent of wages for six months) to hire the unemployed worker.

What if an unemployed worker needs to move to find a job? For this purpose, mobility grants are available, and no less than 10 percent of all job referrals are to jobs in another county (and 37 percent to jobs at another unemployment office).

If all else fails, there is the possibility of temporary public employment (for six months). After 14 months of unemployment, this becomes a legal right.

WHAT CAN WE LEARN FROM SWEDEN?

The United States is not going to adopt Sweden's entire employment strategy in an effort to reform our UI program. However, we can learn several important lessons from the Swedish system. The Swedish system does several things quite well. First, the Swedish employment centers and counselors therein do an excellent job of accumulating and disseminating information on available jobs and available workers. The United States has no similar program. As stated earlier, Swedish job centers have a nationwide, integrated database of jobs, employers, and even available employees that is continually updated and readily available.

Virtually all state-run unemployment insurance organizations in the United States have services to help job seekers find employment, but a database containing a list of jobs nationwide is not available. The United States could set up such a database by requiring that all firms paying unemployment insurance taxes also report bona fide job openings and employment needs. The federal government could then maintain a computerized database of all job openings. State job service agencies could access this database and make such information available to the unemployed.

The United States is obviously not nearly as small nor as homogeneous as Sweden. But a national database of job openings could easily be made part of the existing unemployment insurance program. This could significantly reduce the amount of time spent by average workers on the unemployment rolls and thereby reduce the overall unemployment rate. In addition, this change may even help employers find the type of workers they need because of the nationwide expansion of the labor market.

Another thing that the Swedish employment centers do well is to strictly require job search activities and to require that if a job is offered, it must be taken, or benefits are cut off. If the suggestion of a nationwide database were adopted, and state unemployment agencies thus gained access to more information about available jobs and the necessary skills required, they could then tighten their job search and job acceptance requirements. They could make clear their intention to strictly cut off benefits to those who refused to meet the requirements. The unemployment insurance system could thus provide not only a carrot but also a stick in its efforts to help the unemployed.

In this regard, we can learn another very important lesson from the Swedish. Their entire philosophy is to keep citizens working. Their integration of training and education into the unemployment program is an example of this philosophy.

At present, the vast majority of job training in the United States is provided by employers. As long as employees have the basic skills needed to learn in an on-the-job training environment, many job skills are best taught by employers. The United States could improve its training and education and thereby move closer to the Swedish philosophy, without creating another giant bureaucracy. The first step would be to eliminate the mess of disorganized, wasteful, and nonfunctioning training programs that now litter the federal bureaucracy. The *Wall Street Journal* recently noted that the federal job training effort now drapes across 14 federal agencies. The poor have 65 separate programs designed to help them with education and job training. Most observers agree that few of these programs work, and the added bureaucracy and duplication of efforts simply waste money.[15] The state unemployment agencies, which are closer to the people and more in touch with local labor market conditions, could take responsibility for helping workers get the training and education necessary to be gainfully employed.

What could state unemployment agencies do in this area? Let's imagine an unemployed individual applies for unemployment benefits after being laid off from a job the skills of which are in very low demand. Let's imagine further that the job prospects of this individual are extremely poor unless he or she is retrained. Let's assume that this individual has the necessary basic skills to be retrained—in other words, he or she is literate and has some basic math skills. Many businesses that may be unwilling to hire this individual because of the associated training costs may change their tune if they don't have to pay all of the training costs. If some of the money now used to fund the myriad of training efforts were made available to the state job service or unemployment agencies, they could offer to offset part of the training costs of any firm that agreed to hire a literate, trainable, but hard-to-place worker.

What if an unemployed individual does not possess the basic skills needed to be trained on the job? A training subsidy provided to firms would not do such an individual any long-term good because, lacking the basic skills, she or he would be untrainable. In this case, the state unemployment agencies should be able to offer individuals incentives to get the basic reading, writing, and math skills required in today's marketplace. Such incentives might include an extension of benefits beyond the current 26 weeks and/or an increase in the benefits just enough to offset the tuition costs of remedial education. If such incentives are offered, the recipient should be required to provide proof of enrollment, attendance, and satisfactory completion of the courses. Of course, the ultimate solution to this type of problem is to build a primary and secondary education system that provides our young people with the basic skills needed to be trained and employed. This would eliminate the need for remedial education in all but a few cases. This important topic was briefly discussed in Chapter 3.

We can obviously learn from the strengths of the Swedish employment strategy. But since 1992, Sweden, too, has fallen on hard times, and unemployment has increased to levels similar to those in other European countries, levels Sweden has not seen for more than 20 years. Does this mean that we should stay as far away from the Swedish approach as possible? No. It means that we must try to understand what Sweden did right and what Sweden did wrong. Let us look at why the Swedish unemployment rate has recently broken out of its former ultralow zone.

Sweden kept its unemployment rate low not only through the employment strategy we have described but also by keeping demand high, by propping up local industry through successive currency devaluations and through a willingness to tolerate relatively high inflation.[16] Throughout the 1980s, Sweden allowed its inflation rate to exceed the average for all of Europe. By 1991, the Swedish government realized that it could no longer continue down that path. It realized that to compete in the world economy, inflation must be kept under control, and its system must be reformed.

Only one part of the Swedish welfare system has been described here. Sweden has carried the concept of a welfare state farther than any other Western, industrialized country. It is widely recognized and accepted that, because of their employment strategy, the Swedes have the most flexible and efficient labor market in Europe. But their economy also carries the highest tax burden and high levels of regulation. The Swedes have found that they cannot compete in the world economy without changing the current cradle-to-grave welfare system that creates high tax burdens, high levels of regulation, and high levels of inflation. We can learn from the things Sweden did right without throwing the baby out with the bathwater.

TAXES AND UNEMPLOYMENT

So far in this chapter we have focused on social welfare programs used by governments to provide a safety net for citizens. What about the taxes necessary to pay for that safety net and, indeed, for all government activities? Can increased taxes lead to higher unemployment?

The answer is yes. If the taxes are borne by businesses, then business costs will increase, and firms will endeavor to pass those increased costs along to consumers in the form of higher prices. This puts upward pressure on inflation, as discussed previously, and results in higher unemployment as government monetary authorities try to control the inflationary pressure. If taxes borne by consumers or workers are increased, then, in effect, their real take-home pay is reduced. If consumer/workers accept this reduction in real pay and do not try to recoup their losses through higher wages, then no pressure is exerted on inflation, and thus unemployment will not necessarily rise. But if consumers do not accept the lower real take-home pay and try to offset the higher tax burden with higher wages, then increased taxes on workers or consumers can spark inflationary pressure and result in more unemployment.

To find out if increases in U.S. taxes have contributed to a higher U.S. NAIRU, we must answer two questions. First, have total taxes increased in the United States? Second, if the total tax burden in the United States has increased, have workers accepted a reduction in real take-home pay or pushed for higher wages?

Joseph A. Pechman, of the Brookings Institution, has conducted perhaps the most thorough analysis of the changing tax burden in the United States.[17] He found that during the period from 1966 to 1985, overall taxes as a percentage of adjusted family income were 25.2 percent in 1966, 26.1 percent in 1970, 25.0 percent in 1975, 25.2 percent in 1980, and 24.5 percent in 1985. In other words, during the time when the U.S. unemployment rate was increasing, the tax burden for all taxpayers did not increase. Looking at effective tax rates by population deciles, Pechman found that, between 1966 and 1985, the tax burdens increased in the two lowest deciles, remained about the same in the third and fourth deciles, rose slightly in the fifth to the ninth deciles, but declined in the highest decile.

What Pechman's analysis tells us is that since the tax burden in the U.S. economy did not increase, taxes could not have been responsible for an increase in the U.S. unemployment rate. Furthermore, Richard Layard has pointed out that in Great Britain, where tax burdens have likely increased, workers accepted the reduction in real take-home pay instead of pushing for higher wages. If, by some chance, Pechman is wrong, and the U.S. tax burden has increased, then U.S. workers may very well have accepted the reduction in real take-home pay as did workers in Great Britain. We can conclude that increases in tax burdens in the U.S. economy have not been a factor in the increase in the U.S. NAIRU.[18]

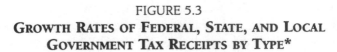

FIGURE 5.3
**GROWTH RATES OF FEDERAL, STATE, AND LOCAL
GOVERNMENT TAX RECEIPTS BY TYPE***

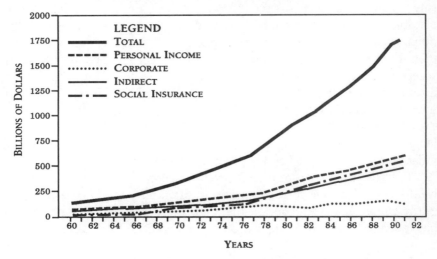

*Source: *Economic Report of the President* (Washington, DC: United States Government Printing Office, Superintendent of Documents, 1993), p. 440.

The analysis of Edmund Phelps's recently published book on taxes and unemployment differs from that previously outlined in one important respect. Phelps argues that it is not the total tax burden that matters but, rather, only payroll taxes. He argues that taxes on consumer expenditures or on production of consumer goods are neutral as far as employment is concerned, but payroll taxes have definite negative impacts on employment. In other words, if payroll taxes increase, even though the total tax burden remains constant, taxes may still push up the unemployment rate.[19]

Figure 5.3 shows the growth rates (log scale) of the various types of federal, state, and local taxes. The figure clearly shows that one type of tax has grown much faster than total taxes and, indeed, faster than any other type of tax, and that is social insurance payroll taxes.

Phelps argues that for the OECD countries, increased payroll taxes contributed to higher unemployment in the mid-1970s to early 1980s and especially in the period from 1981 to 1989.

If Phelps's analysis is correct, then one thing the United States and, indeed, other countries as well can do is to cut back on social welfare programs that require payroll taxes. This should allow a cut in payroll taxes and, according to Phelps's analysis, a reduction in the NAIRU.

CONCLUSIONS AND RECOMMENDATIONS

Many European countries offer unemployment and social welfare benefits that are much more generous than those of the United States. These countries not only provide more money per individual but also allow individuals to collect benefits almost indefinitely. For the most part, analysts agree that such programs contribute greatly to unemployment in general and to long-term unemployment in particular.

The U.S. unemployment insurance program obviously does not have the same impact as do more generous and time-unlimited programs. But during the period from 1960 to 1980, social welfare benefits as a whole grew significantly and probably contributed to an increase in the U.S. NAIRU. During the early 1990s, however, the per-person dollar value of some public assistance programs declined. This decline may have contributed to a decline in the U.S. NAIRU. Edmund Phelps suggests that the decline in the per-person dollar value of public-assistance programs increased work incentives and helped reduce the NAIRU from 6.5 percent to 6 percent.[20]

This chapter has argued that the U.S. social welfare system can be improved further. The United States can learn from both the bad example of some European countries and the good example of others, specifically Sweden. The employment philosophy of the Swedish unemployment system contains several things that the United States could incorporate into its unemployment insurance system. First, information flows could be improved. Second, job search and acceptance requirements could be tightened and more strictly enforced. Third, the United States could improve its education system and encourage the already existing system of employer-based on-the-job training.

The entire welfare system in the United States needs to be overhauled. It provides too many disincentives for work and too many incentives to blame the system. Any overhaul should keep in mind the lessons taught by the European system of social welfare benefits—namely, that overly generous, open-ended benefits simply result in more and longer-lasting unemployment. What can we suggest about welfare reform?

First, our current system of welfare is not working. We may have won the cold war, but in the War on Poverty, poverty won. By 1985, the federal government spent six times more in constant dollars on 59 federal welfare programs than was spent on all state and federal welfare programs in 1960. Yet, the portion of the U.S. population living in poverty has remained virtually constant, while the percentage of children living in single parent homes has skyrocketed.[21]

Welfare reform is needed. Both conservatives and liberals agree. This consensus on the need for welfare reform is not new. In fact, conservatives and liberals have, for a number of years, agreed that welfare reform is needed. But conservatives have typically argued that too much money is being spent on welfare, and the amount should be reduced, and liberals have typically argued that not enough money is being spent, and the amount should be increased. Some analysts are now arguing that a consensus is emerging that is being embraced by both conservatives and liberals.

On the subject of consensus in welfare reform, James S. Denton has pointed out that, at the most basic level, the consensus is that a welfare system that spends money better can be built. The primary features of this system would include making the clearest possible distinction between people who can and cannot fend for themselves; developing governmental policies that assure a decent standard of living for those who cannot fend for themselves; and developing policies that provide assistance and stern incentives for those who can fend for themselves to get them into the workforce and stable families and keep them there.[22]

According to Robert Reischauer, the emerging welfare reform consensus centers on five broad themes: responsibility, work, family, education, and state discretion.[23] Let us outline what these themes entail.

Responsibility can be contrasted with entitlement. Welfare recipients should know that they are not simply entitled to help because they are poor. They have obligations to work and to strive to become self-sufficient. In this regard, "workfare" is becoming more popular. Workfare means that all able-bodied recipients will be required to prepare themselves for employment, look for jobs, and accept jobs if offered. If this fails, recipients will be required to accept a public job in return for their welfare check.

The consensus on work reflects partly the traditional value placed on work in a liberal capitalist society. It also reflects a change in attitudes toward working mothers. Most Americans now accept the idea that it is appropriate and perhaps even desirable for mothers to work outside the home.

The consensus on family issues is related to the dramatic changes that have taken place in the composition of the American family and the number of women and children living in poverty. Related and contributing to these changes are the increase in divorce, the increase in the number of children living in single-parent households and/or born out of wedlock, and so on. Little consensus exists on how to reduce out-of-wedlock births or single-parent homes, but there is a strong consensus on strengthening parental financial responsibility (especially paternal)—in other words, child-support mechanisms.

The consensus on education is fairly simple and straightforward. Educational failure leads to welfare dependency. Public schools need to be reformed. There is even talk of requiring teenage welfare mothers to graduate from high school.

The final area of consensus identified by Reischauer is that states should have more control over their own welfare policies and programs. States exhibit a great diversity as to the range of people who need welfare support, labor market conditions, educational systems, and so on. In addition, a fair amount of experimentation in welfare reform has occurred at the state level, and conservatives and liberals alike are beginning to applaud these efforts and recognize that welfare programs need to be sensitive to local conditions.

Looking at welfare reform strictly with an eye to improving the unemployment situation, which parts of the welfare reform consensus can we recommend? In general, any reform that strengthens work incentives and/or removes incentives to simply pick up a benefit check without obligation would help improve the unemployment situation. (Here we refer also to those who are able-bodied and capable of work but may not technically be unemployed due to having dropped out of the labor force in order to collect welfare benefits.)

The idea of introducing more responsibility and obligations into welfare benefit systems would strengthen work incentives and could be recommended on an unemployment basis. The idea of requiring those benefit recipients who can work to do so is part of the same package. Increasing parental, especially paternal, financial responsibility for children, if properly done, would also increase work incentives and perhaps help reduce unemployment.

We have already discussed how important a quality educational system is to keeping unemployment low. If improving public schools is also part of welfare reform, then it comes doubly recommended.

State discretion is not as clear-cut. If state discretion results in reforms that reduce reservation wages and increase work incentives, then state discretion will result in a lower unemployment rate. But if, on average, state discretion increases reservation wages and/or reduces work incentives in the United States, then the unemployment rate will increase. There is, however, ample reason to believe that state discretion, on average, will result in welfare reforms that emphasize the other parts of the welfare reform consensus. To date, states have been at the forefront of introducing such programs as workfare and increased parental financial responsibility. More state discretion would likely result in more experimentation in these and other areas that will, over time, help reduce the U.S. unemployment rate. We say "over time" because, as states experiment with new programs, some will work and some will not. Those that work will be copied. Competition between states will lead to the best programs gaining widespread acceptance. With welfare policy being dictated from the national government, very little experimentation and competition can occur.[24]

In summary, virtually all of the parts of the welfare reform consensus identified by Reischauer have the potential to help reduce the U.S. unemployment rate. We therefore recommend that welfare reform incorporating this consensus be enacted.

NOTES

1. *Wall Street Journal*, May 12, 1993, p. A14.

2. See Murray Rubin, "Federal-State Relations in Unemployment Insurance," in W. Lee Hansen and James F. Byers (eds.), *Unemployment Insurance: The Second Half-Century* (Madison: University of Wisconsin Press, 1990).

3. *Report to the President of the Committee on Economic Security* (Washington, DC: Government Printing Office, 1935).

4. Richard K. Vedder and Lowell E. Gallaway, *Out of Work: Unemployment and Government in Twentieth-Century America* (New York: Holmes & Meier, 1993).

5. Ibid.

6. David R. Henderson, "The Europeanization of the U.S. Labor Market," *Public Interest* 113 (Fall 1993), pp. 66-81.

7. Ibid.

8. Ibid.

9. International Monetary Fund, *World Economic Outlook* (Washington, DC: IMF, May 1994), p. 36.

10. Lawrence F. Katz and Bruce D. Meyer, "The Impact of the Potential Duration of Unemployment Benefits on the Duration of Unemployment,"

Journal of Public Economics 41 (1990), pp. 45-72.

11. For a more complete discussion of the Swedish system, see Richard Layard and John Philpott, *Stopping Unemployment* (London: The Employment Institute, 1991).

12. Ibid.

13. Ibid.

14. Ibid.

15. *Wall Street Journal*, December 16, 1993, p. 1.

16. *Economist*, February 22, 1992, p. 44.

17. Joseph A. Pechman, *Who Paid Taxes, 1966-85?* (Washington, DC: Brookings Institution, 1985).

18. Richard Layard, *How to Beat Unemployment* (Oxford, England: Oxford University Press, 1986).

19. Edmund S. Phelps, *Structural Slumps: The Modern Equilibrium Theory of Unemployment, Interest, and Assets* (Cambridge, MA: Harvard University Press, 1994).

20. Amanda Bennett, "Business and Academia Clash over a Concept: 'Natural' Jobless Rate," *Wall Street Journal*, January 24, 1995, p. 1.

21. James S. Denton, *Welfare Reform: Consensus or Conflict?* (Lanham, MD: University Press of America, 1988).

22. "Introduction," Denton, *Welfare Reform*.

23. Robert Reischauer, "The Welfare Reform Legislation: Direction for the Future," in P. Cottingham and D. Ellwood (eds.), *Welfare Policy for the 1990s* (Cambridge: Harvard University Press, 1989), pp. 10-40.

24. For a more complete discussion, see Garry K. Ottosen, *Making American Government Work: A Proposal to Reinvigorate Federalism* (Lanham, MD: University Press of America, 1992).

CHAPTER 6

The Union Wage Premium and the NAIRU

W hat have we found so far about the NAIRU? First, the jobs summit with its focus on mismatch unemployment and its emphasis on training and retraining as a solution, at best, looked at only a small part of the picture. An increase in mismatch unemployment has not been shown to be the major reason the NAIRU has increased. Second, business costs have increased. The oil price shocks and other shocks in the 1970s caused business costs to go up dramatically, but these shocks could only have temporarily increased the NAIRU since they have, by and large, been reversed. Government-imposed costs in the form of regulations have also increased dramatically, and these cost increases have not been reversed. In fact, they appear to be increasing. This imposed-cost factor may very well be linked to the higher U.S. NAIRU. Third, unemployment insurance and welfare payments can lead to more unemployment. Changes in these programs may also have contributed to a higher NAIRU. Reform of these programs may also significantly reduce unemployment.

This chapter looks at another factor that may have contributed to an increase in the U.S. NAIRU. It examines the effect labor unions have on business costs through their effect on wages and benefits.

By increasing the relative wages and/or benefits of union workers, labor unions increase business costs and reduce the amount of labor that employers can use profitably. In addition, workers who are laid off from relatively high-wage union jobs will have high reservation wages. That is, because they are accustomed to a relatively high wage (an uncompetitive wage), they will be reluctant to quickly accept jobs that pay competitive wages and will choose to be unemployed for longer periods of time while they search for a job that pays wages close to their previous union-inflated wage level. Union-induced high reservation wages reduce the effectiveness of unemployment in combatting inflation because unemployed workers with high reservation wages compete less vigorously for jobs than workers who do not have such high reservation wages. Thus, they exert less downward pressure on wage levels. A higher level of unemployment is then necessary to control inflation than would otherwise be the case.

Virtually all analysts of labor unions agree that unions do raise the *relative* wages of their members. Likewise, virtually all analysts agree that unions also raise the *reservation* wages of unemployed union members. But these two arguments do not necessarily mean that unions have contributed to the rising U.S. unemployment rate. To determine if unions have played any role in the worsening unemployment situation, we must examine the extent of unionization in the United States, changes in the extent of unionization, the level of the union wage premium, changes in the union wage premium, and whether or not a significant spillover from union wages to nonunion wages exists.

Why are these issues important? Why is it not enough to simply point out the thoroughly analyzed fact that unions raise the relative wages of their members? First, an unchanging union wage premium cannot cause an increasing unemployment rate unless the extent of unionization increases. For example, let's say that before the passage of the National Labor Relations Act (NLRA) in 1935, unions did not have the monopoly power necessary to extract from employers a union wage premium. In other words, union members earned competitive wages. Let's further assume that within a short period of time after passage of the NLRA, union members were able to demand and receive a 15 percent union wage premium; in other words, the wages of union members were, on average, 15 percent higher than they would have been absent the union influence wages. This increase in union wages could have caused a onetime increase in the unemployment rate at the time it occurred. But if the union wage premium remained at 15 percent, and the percentage of workers belonging to unions stayed the same, then high union relative wages could not account for any further increases in the unemployment rate. If, however, either the union wage premium or the percent unionized continued to increase, then the unemployment rate would increase as well, and the blame could properly be laid at the feet of the union wage premium.

THE UNION WAGE PREMIUM

Table 6.1 contains several authors' estimates of the union wage premium over time. What is the union wage premium? It is the premium that union workers earn over comparable nonunion workers generally expressed in percentage terms. For example, a union wage premium of 30 percent means that, for otherwise comparable positions, a union worker makes 30 percent more than a nonunion worker. In column 1 we note that George Johnson has argued that the union wage premium was around 25 percent in the early 1960s. According to his estimates, it declined to around 19 percent by 1970 and then increased through the 1970s to about 30 percent by 1980.[1]

H. Gregg Lewis has authored perhaps more work on the union wage premium than any other economist. In his 1986 book *Union Relative Wage Effects*, he analyzed more than 100 separate studies of the union wage premium, corrected them for obvious errors, and attempted to standardize the results. Column 2 lists his estimates of the union wage premium between 1967 and 1979. His work, like that of George Johnson, reveals that the union wage premium increased significantly in the 1970s.[2]

The third, fourth, and fifth columns of Table 6.1 show very rough estimates of the union wage premium from a 1989 study by Michael Wachter and William Carter. The column 3 estimates are simply the ratio between union wages as measured by the Major Collective Bargaining Agreements series put out by the Bureau of Labor Statistics (BLS) and nonunion wages as measured by average hourly earnings in industries that had very low percentages of unionization. Column 4 estimates the union wage premium by comparing earnings in industries with very high levels of unionization with earnings in industries with very low levels of unionization. Column 5 lists Wachter and Carter's estimates of the union wage premium based on data from the Employment Cost Index (ECI). This data should be superior to the other two series because separate data on union and nonunion wages are collected, but they go back only to 1976. The ratio in column 5 has as its numerator union wages as measured by the BLS Major Collective Bargaining Agreements series; the denominator is nonunion and nonexecutive wages as measured by the ECI series.[3]

Although the estimates of the union wage premium in columns 3, 4, and 5 are significantly higher than Gregg Lewis' estimates, they show a similar pattern. They also suggest a significant increase in the union wage premium during the 1970s. In addition, these numbers show that the premium has not declined appreciably in the 1980s.

The numbers in columns 6 and 7 are also from Michael Wachter and William Carter but are from a separate 1990 paper.[4] Column 6 contains estimates of the union wage premium from a standard regression-type

analysis of current population survey data such as is often found in the
literature. The model used simply compares union wages with nonunion

TABLE 6.1
ESTIMATES OF THE UNION WAGE PREMIUM OVER TIME

	1	2	3	4	5	6	7
YEAR	GEORGE H. JOHNSON	GREGG LEWIS	WACHTER & CARTER	WACHTER & CARTER	WACHTER & CARTER	WACHTER & CARTER	WACHTER & CARTER
1960	25		26.7	32.6			
1961			26.5	32.5			
1962			25	31.4			
1963			24.3	30.6			
1964			23.5	29.4			
1965			22.1	28			
1966			20.3	26.3			
1967		11	19.1	24			
1968		11	18.3	23.5			
1969		11	17.6	22.5			
1970	19	12	20.7	1.2			
1971		15	24	22.3			
1972		12	24.3	24.9			
1973		15	25.7	26.3		15.5	20.5
1974		14	29.7	26.9		14.6	20.4
1975		16	30.1	0.4		16	21.6
1976		18	32	33.7	31	16.6	21.8
1977		17	32.7	35.3	32.8	17.9	23
1978		17	32.7	35.9	33.2	16.8	22.6
1979		13	34.6	37.2	33.6	12.3	17.7
1980	30		36.2	38	36.9	14.9	20.1
1981			37.3	39.9	39.2	13.9	19.6
1982			37.5	40.4	40.7		
1983			35.1	39.3	39.8	15.5	21.4
1984			35.5	39.8	39.6	16.6	22.2
1985			35.6	40.1	37.4	16.1	21.2
1986			34.6	38.7	35.9	16.1	21.5
1987			34.7	37	35.8		
1988			32.5	35	32.6		
1989			31	32.8	31.3		

wages of workers in the *same industry* after controlling for worker characteristics and other variables. The numbers in column 6 are comparable to Lewis's estimates in column 2.

Wachter and Carter argue that comparing union wages with nonunion wages within the same industry may not provide an accurate estimate of the union wage premium. They point out that threat effects may cause nonunion sectors in highly unionized industries to pay noncompetitive wage rates. Thus within-industry type analyses may understate the true union wage premium. They argue that a better estimate would compare the union wage in each industry to the wage these workers could expect to receive if they lost their union jobs. Column 7 in our table shows Wachter and Carter's estimate of the union wage premium based on this "opportunity wage" concept.

Columns 6 and 7 show only Wachter and Carter's *average* union wage premium estimates. Their more detailed analysis, based on sectors, clearly shows that union wage premiums increased significantly across a broad spectrum of industries between 1973 and 1986, particularly in sectors where the premiums were already high. Their analysis also shows that, in construction, finance, and services, the premiums were stable or declining.

None of the estimates listed in Table 6.1 considered fringe benefits. As discussed later in this chapter, the union effect on fringe benefits is thought to be greater in percentage terms than the union wage premium.

The various estimates listed in Table 6.1 are not the only available estimates of changes in the union wage premium over the period from 1960 to 1990. For instance, in a 1986 study, Richard B. Freeman used Current Population Survey (CPS) data to estimate the premium during the period from 1973 to 1984. He found that the union wage premium increased significantly between 1973 (19 percent) and 1978 (23 percent). The premium then declined to about its 1973 level during the period from 1979 to 1983 but increased again in 1984 (22 percent).[5]

A study by Barry T. Hirsch and John L. Neufeld in 1987, also using CPS data, supports Freeman's results for the period from 1973 to 1983.[6] A study by Michael A. Curme and David A. MacPherson extended the results of Hirsch and Neufeld to cover the period from 1979 to 1988. They found that the union wage premium was higher in 1983-85 (19 percent) than in 1979-81 (14 percent) and that the union wage premium declined only slightly between 1985 and 1988 in spite of falling unionization.[7]

What can we conclude from the literature on changes in the union wage premium? One thing that seems evident is that the union wage premium increased significantly during the 1970s. No matter which methodology is used to analyze the union wage premium, virtually all studies find that it increased in the 1970s. Most studies find that the premium was lower during the period from 1979 to 1981 but went back up in the period from 1983 to 1985 and has not declined by much since then.

UNION DENSITY

Could this increasing union wage premium help explain the increase in the U.S. NAIRU? Before we can answer that, we must examine what

TABLE 6.2

UNION MEMBERSHIP AS A PROPORTION OF NONFARM EMPLOYMENT*

YEAR	PERCENT UNION		
		1976	24.5
1960	31.5	1977	24.1
1961	30.2	1978	24.0
1962	29.9	1979	23.6
1963	29.2	1980	23.2
1964	28.9	1981	22.2
1965	28.5	1982	21.2
1966	28.1	1983	20.3
1967	27.9	1984	19.0
1968	27.9	1985	18.3
1969	27.0	1986	17.8
1970	27.3	1987	17.3
1971	27.0	1988	17.0
1972	26.4	1989	16.6
1973	25.9	1990	16.3
1974	25.8	1991	16.3
1975	25.3	1992	16.0

*Sources: For the years 1960-78, see U.S. Department of Labor, Bureau of Labor Statistics, *Directory of National Unions and Employee Associations*, Bulletin 2079, 1979. For the years 1979-82, see Leo Troy and Neil Sheflin, *Union Sourcebook* (West Orange, NJ: Industrial Relations Data and Information Services, 1985). For the years 1983-92, see U.S. Department of Labor, Bureau of Labor Statistics, "Union Members in 1983 [and other years]."

has happened to the union sphere of influence. In other words, we must find out what proportion of all workers are affected by the union wage premium and if that proportion has changed. If a large percentage of all workers have their earnings affected by the union wage premium, then an increase in it could cause significant unemployment problems. If, however, only a small percentage of all workers have their earnings affected by the union wage premium, then an increase would cause only minor unemployment problems.

Table 6.2 shows the proportion of all nonfarm workers who were union members between 1960 and 1992. In 1960, nearly one-third of all nonfarm workers belonged to labor unions. By 1992, fewer than one-sixth did. Most of the decline in unionization occurred in the 1980s. Between 1980 and 1992, the unionization rate among nonfarm employees declined by more than seven percentage points. During the 1970s, unionization declined by only a relatively modest three percentage points. Throughout the 1970s, when the union wage premium was increasing dramatically, unions represented more than 25 percent of all nonfarm workers. The union sphere of influence was undoubtedly larger than this due to spillover and threat effects, a topic to which we now turn.

UNION WAGE SPILLOVER

Unions not only affect the wages of their members but also may affect the wages of many nonunion workers. For instance, unions may force nonunion companies to raise wages to the union level in order to keep their workers satisfied enough that they feel no need for union representation. This is often called the "threat effect." The economic literature, while not conclusive, seems to indicate that unions do raise the wages of nonunion workers in highly organized industries.[8] Unions also seem to raise the wages of white-collar workers in firms where blue-collar workers are organized. But spillover does not seem to occur from union wages in general to nonunion wages in general. In other words, unions appear to have a sphere of influence within which they can deliver a wage premium. That sphere includes, of course, union members and many nonunion workers in highly organized industries that may be tempted to organize if they are not paid union wages, as well as white-collar workers within organized firms. The union sphere of influence is smaller in industries that are traditionally nonunion and consist mainly of small companies.[9]

Spillover is important because if it exists, then the union wage premium must apply to more than just union workers. Union wage levels can be quite visible and well publicized, and employers may feel pressure to match those levels or at least come close to them. The closer to the union sphere of influence a company is, the more pressure it is likely to feel to match union wages.

Richard Freeman and James Medoff in their oft-cited book *What Do Unions Do?* argue that *large* nonunion firms are heavily influenced by union wage rates.[10] That is, most large nonunion firms are close to, if not in, the union sphere of influence. This is, at least partly, because such companies make extensive use of surveys of average wage levels in their industries and localities as guides to setting wages. Union wage increases raise the rate of pay within these surveys and thus provide an avenue for union wage increases to spill over into nonunion wage increases. A study by Fred K. Foulkes of large nonunion firms provides numerous examples of large nonunion firms copying union wages in setting their own wage rates.[11] Freeman and Medoff argue that unionism probably raises the wages of workers in large nonunion firms by a substantial 10-20 percent and improves benefits as well.[12]

Several factors seem to indicate that union wage spillover might have been larger in the past than it is now. The administrative sector, as Daniel J. B. Mitchell has called it, was much larger during the 1960s and 1970s than it was in the 1980s or at the present.[13] The administrative sector is characterized by big firms, big unions, and bureaucratic personnel policies. This chapter has already pointed out that large nonunion employers, the type of employers that would be part of Mitchell's administrative sector, are much more susceptible to spillover from union wages than smaller nonunion firms. Firms in the administrative sector were not only more important in terms of employment in the 1970s but also more visible and perhaps carried more prestige than in the 1980s. Large U.S. firms still dominated many of the world's industries. This visibility and prestige made spillover from wage increases in this sector to wage increases in other sectors more likely.

One other factor may have significantly affected spillover during the 1970s. The 1970s can accurately be called the COLA age of union contracts. During this period, virtually all of the major unions fought for, and obtained, long-term contracts that contained generous cost-of-living adjustments (COLAs). These COLAs guaranteed that real wages would not decline as a result of unanticipated inflation. Wallace E. Hendricks and Lawrence M. Kahn in their book on cost-of-living adjustments have shown that, in 1966, only 20 percent of the workers in the BLS's Major

Collective Bargaining Agreements series had COLAs. By 1977, this percentage had increased to 61.2 percent. They also show that the agreed-upon COLAs were more liberal in this period than in the past.[14] The big push for COLAs that occurred during this period was the direct result of unions having been burned by unanticipated inflation in earlier periods.

Many analysts of changes in the union wage premium attribute its dramatic rise to the combination of widespread COLAs in long-term union contracts and supply shocks. This view is supported by the fact that the union wage premium did not increase during the 1970s in the construction industry, an industry characterized by short-term contracts and few COLAs.[15]

As COLAs spread throughout the union sector and the visible administrative sector, they became an easy device to spread wage increases to other sectors. In an era of relatively high and uncertain inflation, COLAs began to be viewed not as a luxury but as a necessity by many employees. COLAs, which originated in the union sector, probably increased spillover during the 1970s. This added to the increase in the union wage premium and probably helped to raise the U.S. unemployment rate.

What can we conclude about spillover? At the very least, spillover brings large nonunion firms within the union sphere of influence. How big is the nonunion, large-firm sector? Unfortunately, the government collects no data on the percentage of total employment in large nonunion firms. But the Small Business Administration has estimated that, in 1982, 54 percent of all employees worked for firms with more than 500 employees.[16] Fifty-four percent probably represents the upper limit of the union sphere of influence. This upper limit assumes a significant spillover effect. The lower limit is simply the percent unionized and assumes no spillover.

THE UNION WAGE PREMIUM AND COSTS

Using the limits mentioned in the last section, we can estimate what effect the union wage premium has on costs in the economy. As noted earlier, the literature on the union wage premium contains estimates of the union wage premium ranging from about 10 percent to more than 30 percent. Let us assume that 10 percent is the lower bound and 30 percent the upper bound. Wages, salaries, and supplements to wages represent about 75 percent of all costs in the economy.[17] To establish what impact the union wage premium has on total costs in the economy we simply multiply the union wage premium expressed as a percentage by the union sphere of influence expressed as a percentage and by wages and salaries as a percentage of total costs. In other words:

UNION EFFECT = UNION WAGE x UNION SPHERE x WAGES & SALARIES
ON COSTS   PREMIUM   OF INFLUENCE   COSTS

As of 1992, we can establish the following limits to the union effect on costs:

UPPER LIMIT = 0.30 X 0.50 X 0.75 = .11
LOWER LIMIT = 0.10 X 0.16 X 0.75 = .01

In other words, the union wage premium increases costs by at least 1 percent and by at most 11 percent. This is obviously quite a range. The true impact probably lies in the lower middle of this range, probably in the area of 4-7 percent. This implies a union wage premium of about 20 to 25 percent and a union sphere of influence of about 25 to 35 percent.

In terms of explaining unemployment, establishing what impact the union wage premium has on costs at a single point in time does not help us very much. What we need to know is whether this impact has changed. Let us review the evidence already presented.

Evidence presented in the preceding paragraphs shows that the union wage premium increased significantly during the 1970s and has probably declined only slightly since then. At the same time, union density declined only slightly in the 1970s, but this decline accelerated in the 1980s. If we assume either no spillover or no change in spillover, then the changes in the union wage premium and union density lead us to the conclusion that the union wage premium was an inflationary force in the 1970s that probably increased the U.S. unemployment rate. This is most simply illustrated by multiplying the union wage premium by union density at different points in time. In 1969, the union wage premium was probably around 12 percent. Union density was about 27 percent. The product of these two numbers is 0.032. By 1978, the union wage premium was probably at least 20 percent, while union density was 24 percent. The product of these two numbers is 0.048. If we assume no spillover and that the ratio of wages, salaries, and supplements to wages remained at a constant 75 percent of total costs, then the union wage premium increased from about 2 percent of costs to more than 3.5 percent of costs.

As outlined previously, we cannot assume that spillover was unimportant. Let us assume that spillover in 1969 brought the union sphere of influence up to a modest 35 percent (27 percent union density plus an extra 8 percent spillover.) Given this assumption, the union wage premium would have added about 3 percent to costs. Let us assume further that by 1978 spillover had increased slightly, for reasons just outlined, to around 12 percent. This together with the 24 percent union density would have left the union sphere of influence virtually unchanged through the 1970s as the union wage premium increased. Given these assumptions, by 1978 the union wage premium would have added more than 5 percent to total costs.

An increase from 3 percent of total costs to 5 percent may not seem like a big increase, but in an economy with a labor force of 100 million persons, 1.5 million people would need to be laid off to make up for the 2 percent increase in costs (assuming that labor costs make up 75 percent of all costs). Thus, the increase in the union wage premium during the 1970s may have added significantly to the U.S. unemployment problem.

FRINGE BENEFITS

Wages are only one aspect of total labor costs that may have increased between 1960 and 1990 and contributed to an increase in the U.S. NAIRU, and wages are only one of the things that unions are concerned with. In this section, we look briefly at fringe benefits, which, when combined with wages and salaries, make up total compensation.

What do we mean by fringe benefits? We can divide fringe benefits into seven categories. First, we have the legally required benefits. These are benefits that employers must, by law, provide their employees, like the employer-paid part of social security, unemployment insurance, and workers' compensation insurance. Second, we have employer-provided retirement and savings plans. Third are the employer-paid life insurance and death benefits. Fourth, we have employer-provided medical insurance and other medically related benefit payments. Fifth are paid rest periods, and sixth are paid vacations, holidays, and other payments for time not worked. Finally, we can lump all other employer-paid benefits into a miscellaneous category.

In the rest of this section we hope to shed some light on two important questions: Have employer-provided fringe benefits increased enough that they may have played a role in the increase in the NAIRU? If employee benefits have increased significantly, have unions been a contributing factor? Let us now look at some numbers on employee benefits.

Figure 6.1 shows employee benefits as a percentage of payroll as calculated by the U.S. Chamber of Commerce.[18] Between 1951 and 1978, employee benefits increased from about 18 percent of payroll to more than 37 percent of payroll. This increase in fringe benefits obviously increased business costs. Much of the increase occurred at a time when U.S. productivity was stagnating, and therefore feasible real wages or feasible real total compensation (wages plus fringe benefits) was also stagnating. This increase in business costs may have played a significant role in increasing the NAIRU.

Figure 6.2 shows a different estimate of employee benefit costs. It shows supplements to wages and salaries as contained in the U.S. National Income and Product Account tables as a percentage of GDP. This figure, like Figure 6.1, shows that employee benefits have increased significantly since the early 1960s. Most of this increase took place during the 1970s.

FIGURE 6.1
**EMPLOYEE BENEFITS AS A
PERCENTAGE OF PAYROLL***

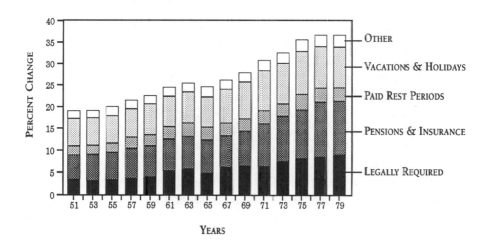

*Source: U.S. Chamber of Commerce, *Employee Benefits Historical Data*, 1981; and U.S. Chamber of Commerce, *Employee Benefits*, various years.

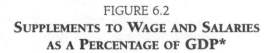

FIGURE 6.2
**SUPPLEMENTS TO WAGE AND SALARIES
AS A PERCENTAGE OF GDP***

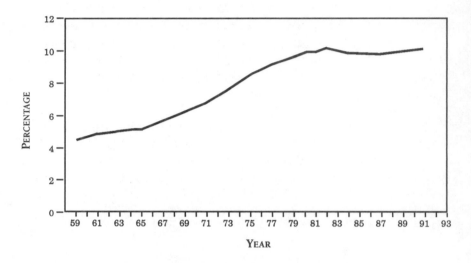

*Source: U.S. National Income and Product Account Tables.

Figure 6.2 also gives us some idea of how important fringe benefits are in the economy. By the 1980s, the cost of fringe benefits amounted to at least 10 percent of GDP. Obviously, they are not unimportant. Some analysts have argued that fringe benefits are now so high that labor is pricing itself out of the market. In other words, companies are increasingly finding it more profitable to employ more capital equipment and less labor.[19] Evidence exists, therefore, that the increase in labor costs due to increasing fringe benefits may have been a contributing factor in the increase in the U.S. NAIRU.

What about unions? Have they played a role in the increasing level of fringe benefits? In recent years, union officials have bought advertising time on radio stations to tell how average workers in America would not have many of the employment benefits that they now have, like health insurance, pensions, vacation time, and others, if unions had not first forced unionized firms to grant them. Even business publications attribute the spread of fringe benefits directly to unionization.[20] It is difficult to know exactly how many of the fringe benefits would have come about and would have spread widely in the absence of unionization, but we do agree with the union line in one respect: most of the employer-provided fringe benefits U.S. workers now enjoy first took hold in the union sector. Unions may not have been the originators of fringe benefits, but they have been at the forefront of securing and protecting those benefits.[21]

The economic literature on the subject of unions and fringe benefits is not nearly as extensive as the literature on unions and wage levels. Yet, it shares with that literature its nearly universal support for a finding of a positive union impact. In general, the literature finds that unions increase not only the availability of fringe benefits but also their level.[22]

Good information regarding *changes* in the union fringe benefit premium is not available to us. Some sources put the *level* of this premium at somewhat higher than the union wage premium. For instance, Freeman and Medoff have argued that it is around 30 percent.[23] Whether this is higher or lower than in the past, we do not know. We do know that fringe benefits have increased in importance in the U.S. economy and have increased business costs. To the extent that unions were responsible for this increase, they may also have been responsible for some of the increase in the NAIRU. This union fringe benefit effect is above and beyond the union impact on the unemployment rate through the union wage premium, and it will increase our estimates of the union impact on the unemployment rate accordingly.

CONCLUSIONS AND RECOMMENDATIONS

Do policies exist that we could now implement to counteract the union wage and fringe benefit premiums' effects and help bring down the U.S. unemployment rate? As already mentioned, union density has declined significantly in the 1980s. Since the administrative sector is not as important now as it once was, union wage spillover is also probably not as important. Thus, the union sphere of influence is probably now more like 20-25 percent rather than the 35-40 percent of the 1970s. Many, after looking at these numbers, would argue that since the union sphere of influence is now shrinking, no policies to counter the union wage premium effect on unemployment are needed. They might argue further that, even though the union wage premium is still high, the decline in the union sphere of influence has already done more than any public policy could hope to do to reduce union influence on average wage levels and thus business costs. The point is well taken. But still, unions enjoy many privileges under current labor law that, given the right circumstances, could again allow them to exert a significant influence on wage levels and thus unemployment. So in order to prevent a repeat of the 1970s, labor law should be changed.

Overhaul the NLRA

Labor unions do not need to be outlawed to effect an adequate change in labor law. But their special privileges do need to be taken away. One way to do this would be to overhaul, but not repeal, the National Labor Relations Act (NLRA) and other labor legislation that currently shields labor unions from the disciplining forces of competition and allows them to deliver monopolistic wage and fringe benefit premiums. In the next chapter, we discuss the NLRA in much more detail and there propose changes to it.

Even if the United States were to take the radical step of repealing the NLRA, labor unions would still be free to organize and represent any workers that wanted such representation. But unions would have to compete with other organizations like company-sponsored organizations, to provide the services desired by workers. Richard A. Epstein in an oft-quoted paper has argued that labor unions do not need the special treatment that they now receive under the NLRA and other labor laws. He outlines how labor unions could continue to function under a sensible common-law regime relying heavily upon tort and contract law. According to Epstein, the tort principles protect individuals against the use of threat of force and the deliberate inducement of breach of contract. The contract principles allow individuals within this special framework of entitlements to make whatever bargains they please with whomever they please.[24] Professor Epstein points out that arguing for repeal of the NLRA is not arguing against unions as such. It is arguing against their special privileges and immunities. "Where unions are necessary to foster communication, they can emerge in any voluntary situation, in a form less formal and less adversarial than it is today."[25] Epstein might also have added that unions can emerge in a form that would not lead to higher target real wages and thus more unemployment.

Repeal the Davis-Bacon Act

Another law that tends to push up target real wages and may therefore have an influence on the unemployment rate is the Davis-Bacon Act.

This law should not be overhauled but repealed. It requires that workers on federally financed construction jobs be paid wages at "local prevailing rates." It was amended in 1964 to include fringe benefits as well as wage rates. The act orders that for every federal construction project exceeding $2,000, the secretary of labor should establish a minimum construction wage, which is the "prevailing wage for a corresponding class of laborer in the city, town, village, or civil subdivision in which the work is to be performed."

Since 1931, Congress has extended the prevailing wage provision to include most federally assisted construction, whether state, local, or national governments are the direct purchasers. The prevailing wage is administratively determined by the Wage and Hour division of the Department of Labor, and minimum wages are set primarily on a project basis.

According to Morgan O. Reynolds, the ambiguity of the prevailing wage concept has given the Department of Labor the latitude to set minimum rates at union rates.[26] Reynolds notes that the Government Accounting Office (GAO) found that in a sample of 73 wage determinations, half were union-negotiated rates. Of 530 area determinations, 302 (57 percent) were union rates rather than determined from wage surveys. The GAO found that the Department of Labor bureaucrats could not compile timely information on a voluntary basis from a multitude of relevant sources.

> The Wage and Hour Division does not use a consistent methodology in its surveys, adds and deletes wage data on an ad hoc basis, includes previous Davis-Bacon projects in the data, adopts arbitrary job classifications, and imports urban wage rates into rural area projects in order to benefit unions. At the very least, the Department of Labor sets the average construction wage rate in an area as the minimum wage rate for particular projects and labor skills and more often sets the union wage as the minimum wage.[27]

For these and other reasons, the GAO in 1979 recommended repeal of the Davis-Bacon Act. This book supports the GAO's recommendation.

Studies on the cost of the act do not agree on how much it raises costs, but virtually all of them do agree that it does raise costs. For instance, the GAO estimated the cost of Davis-Bacon in 1977 at more than $500 million in extra labor costs, plus $189 million in administrative costs borne by contractors and $12 million incurred by federal agencies, for a total cost of more than $700 million. The U.S. Chamber of Commerce, on the other hand, estimated the total cost of Davis-Bacon at $2.8 billion a year, including direct costs of $1 billion and indirect costs of $1.8 billion.[28]

A 1984 paper by Martha Norby Fraundorf, John P. Farrell, and Robert Mason found that Davis-Bacon increased total construction costs in rural areas by 26.1 percent.[29] The authors do not mention a percentage for urban areas, but it is presumably lower. We must keep in mind that 20 percent of all construction in the United States is regulated by Davis-Bacon.[30]

A 1986 paper by John F. O'Connell found that Davis-Bacon increases average wages by between 13.13 percent and 32.5 percent.[31] O'Connell also found that Davis-Bacon raises average union wages within geographical areas by enhancing the unions' bargaining position. Thus, he argues that the effect of Davis-Bacon is twofold: nonunion workers are paid a wage higher than they would receive otherwise, and the union wage is higher because of the enhanced bargaining position of the union. The latter effect helps explain labor's adamant support of Davis-Bacon.

Originally, Congress passed the Davis-Bacon Act in response to complaints about the loss of federal construction contracts to itinerant, low-wage contractors. Supporters maintained that requiring all contractors to pay local wages would protect local living standards, provide equal opportunity for local contractors, and stabilize the construction industry.[32] Its effects have been to raise construction costs, enhance union power, keep minority-owned businesses out of federal construction (according to some),[33] and probably to contribute to a high NAIRU. It is past time to repeal this law.

NOTES

1. George Johnson, as cited in Richard B. Freeman and James L. Medoff, *What Do Unions Do?* (New York: Basic Books, 1984), p. 53.

2. H. Gregg Lewis, *Union Relative Wage Effects: A Survey* (Chicago: University of Chicago Press, 1986), p. 186, Table 9.7.

3. Michael L. Wachter and William H. Carter, "Norm Shifts in Union Wages: Will 1989 Be a Replay of 1969?" *Brookings Papers on Economic Activity* 2 (1989), pp. 233-64.

4. Michael L. Wachter and William H. Carter, "Evaluating the Evidence on Union Employment and Wages," *Industrial and Labor Relations Review* 44

(October 1990), pp. 34-53.

5. Richard B. Freeman, "In Search of Union Wage Concessions in Standard Data Sets," *Industrial Relations* 25 (Spring 1986), pp. 131-45.

6. Barry T. Hirsch and John L. Neufeld, "Nominal and Real Union Wage Differentials and the Effects of Industry and SMSA Density," *Journal of Human Resources* 22 (Winter 1987), pp. 138-48.

7. Michael A. Curme and David A. MacPherson, "Union Wage Differentials and the Effects of Industry and Local Union Density: Evidence from the 1980s," *Journal of Labor Research* 12 (Fall 1991), pp. 419-2

8. Michael Podgursky, "Unions, Establishment Size, and Intra-Industry Threat Effects," *Industrial and Labor Relations Review* 39 (January 1986), pp. 277-84.

9. Ibid.

10. Richard Freeman and James Medoff, *What Do Unions Do?* (New York: Basic Books, 1984).

11. Fred K. Foulkes, *Personnel Policies in Large Nonunion Companies* (Englewood Cliffs, NJ: Prentice-Hall, 1980).

12. Freeman and Medoff, *What Do Unions Do?*

13. Daniel J. B. Mitchell, "Wage Pressures and Labor Shortages: The 1960s and 1980s," *Brookings Papers on Economic Activity* 2 (1989), pp. 191-231.

14. Wallace E. Hendricks and Lawrence M. Kahn, *Wage Indexation in the United States: Cola or Uncola* (Cambridge, MA: Ballinger, 1985).

15. Wachter and Carter, "Norm Shifts in Union Wages."

16. Charles Brown, Jones Hamilton, and James Medoff, *Employers Large and Small* (Cambridge: Harvard University Press, 1990).

17. Albert Rees, *The Economics of Trade Unions*, 3d ed. (Chicago: University of Chicago Press, 1989), p. 95.

18. U.S. Chamber of Commerce, *Employee Benefits Historical Data*, 1981; and U.S. Chamber of Commerce, *Employee Benefits*, various years.

19. Lucinda Harper, "Businesses Prefer Buying Equipment to Hiring New Staff," *Wall Street Journal*, September 3, 1993.

20. For example, Aaron Bernstein, "Why America Needs Unions But Not the Kind It Has Now," *Business Week*, May 23, 1994, p. 70-82.

21. Robert M. McCaffery, *Managing the Employee Benefits Program* (New York: America Management Association, 1983).

22. For example, Richard B. Freeman, "The Effect of Unionism on Fringe Benefits," *Industrial and Labor Relations Review* 34 (July 1981), pp. 489-509; Freeman and Medoff, *What Do Unions Do?*; Augustin Kwasi Fosu, "Unions and Fringe Benefits: Additional Evidence," *Journal of Labor Research* 5 (Summer 1984), pp. 247-54; William E. Even and David A. Macpherson, "The Impact of

Unionism on Fringe Benefit Coverage," *Economics Letters* 36 (1991), pp. 87-91; and Augustin Kwasi Fosu, "Nonwage Benefits as a Limited-Dependent Variable: Implications for the Impact of Unions," *Journal of Labor Research* 24 (Winter 1993), pp. 29-43.

23. Freeman and Medoff, *What Do Unions Do?*

24. Richard A. Epstein, "A Common Law for Labor Relations: A Critique of the New Deal Labor Legislation," *Yale Law Journal* 92 (July 1983), pp. 1357-1408.

25. Ibid., p. 1406.

26. Morgan O. Reynolds, "Understanding Political Pricing of Labor Services: The Davis-Bacon Act," *Journal of Labor Research* 3 (Summer 1982), pp. 295-309.

27. Ibid., p. 298.

28. Ibid., p. 300.

29. Martha Norby Fraundorf, John P. Farrell, and Robert Mason, "The Effect of the Davis-Bacon Act on Construction Costs in Rural

Areas," *Review of Economics and Statistics* 66 (February 1984), pp.

142-46.

30. Reynolds, "Understanding Political Pricing."

31. ohn F. O'Connell, "The Effects of Davis-Bacon on Labor Costs and Union Wages," *Journal of Labor Research* 7 (Summer 1986), pp. 239-253.

32. Fraundorf, Farrell, and Mason, "The Effect of Davis-Bacon," p. 142.

33. Scott Alan Hodge, "Davis-Bacon: Racist Then, Racist Now," *Wall Street Journal*, June 25, 1990, p. A14; Nona M. Brazier, "Stop Law That Hurts My Minority Business," *Wall Street Journal*, January 12, 1994, p. A10.

CHAPTER 7

UNION PRODUCTIVITY EFFECTS, LABOR LAW, AND THE NAIRU

U nion effects on wages and fringe benefits are not the only ways unions can increase the NAIRU or the rate of unemployment that is consistent with stable inflation. If, by reducing productivity growth, unions increase business costs, then this will increase the NAIRU through the same mechanism whereby other increased business costs, like government regulation-imposed costs, increase the NAIRU.

Do unions reduce productivity growth? Or do unions increase productivity growth? If unions increase productivity growth, then they may actually offset the union wage premium discussed in the previous chapter. What does the economic literature have to say on this issue?

THE LITERATURE ON UNIONS AND PRODUCTIVITY

When most people think of unions and productivity, they think of union work rules, featherbedding, and other inefficient union practices that would seem to reduce productivity. But beginning with a study by Charles Brown and James Medoff in 1978, several studies have claimed that unions may actually increase the productivity of firms that they organize. These studies argue that unions may boost productivity, first, by "shocking" management into adopting more efficient techniques and, second, by acting as a "collective voice" of workers.

The group of studies that kicked off the union-productivity debate is sometimes referred to as the Harvard studies. Brown and Medoff's paper was the first of the Harvard studies.[1] Their approach differed from the conventional monopoly model view of unions in substance and result. Contrary to the restrictive (productivity-inhibiting) monopoly model, in this new model unions are seen as an institutional force acting as a collective voice of workers and boosting productivity by reducing labor turnover, enhancing worker morale and cooperation, providing efficient grievance resolution, and pressuring management into stricter efficiency. Supportive empirical evidence has been reported in papers by Frantz; Brown and Medoff; Clark; Brown, Freeman, and Leonard (reported in Freeman and Medoff); Connerton, Freeman, and Medoff; and Allen.[2] All of these studies are used in Freeman and Medoff's book *What Do Unions Do?* to support the argument of positive union productivity effects. Two additional studies by Allen and Mefford also suggest that unions have a positive impact on productivity.[3]

Brown and Medoff's study was a cross-sectional analysis of 20 Standard Industrial Classification (SIC) two-digit manufacturing industries, using 1972 data. After controlling for capital per unit of labor and labor force quality, Brown and Medoff estimated that union establishments are 22 percent more productive than nonunion establishments. Frantz found a similar result of a 15 percent positive union effect in a study of the household furniture industry, using 1975-76 data. Brown, Medoff, and Leonard found 10 and 27 percent positive effects using 1972 and 1977 manufacturing data. In two studies of the cement industry, Clark found positive union productivity effects of between 6 and 10 percent. Allen conducted a cross-sectional analysis of the construction industry, using 1972 data, and found a positive union productivity effect of 17 to 22 percent. These studies are the basis of the Freeman and Medoff assertion that unions have productivity effects of similar magnitude to, and that offset, their relative wage effect.

An additional study cited by Freeman and Medoff (conducted by Connerton, Freeman, and Medoff) found seemingly contrary evidence. In separate yearly studies of the bituminous coal industry, they found positive union productivity effects in 1965 but negative effects in 1970 and thereafter. Freeman and Medoff conclude that this negative effect can be attributed to poor labor-management relations in the later time period. Because of the extenuating circumstances, they believe this result does not reject the positive union productivity effect previously postulated.

The second Allen study in this area addressed the union/nonunion productivity issue using a sample of union and nonunion contractors working on privately and publicly owned hospital and nursing home projects. The results of this study were consistent with his earlier findings. Allen again found union productivity to be greater than nonunion productivity. But the empirical results of this study were rather weak, as the null hypothesis of no union/nonunion productivity difference could be rejected at only an 87 percent confidence level.

Mefford examined the effect of unions on productivity in thirty-one plants of a large multinational firm in the years 1975-82. Results of his study indicate that unionization's overall effect on productivity is positive. Unionization appears to increase the capital-labor ratio and improve management performance, but it also raises the absenteeism rate. A net positive effect on productivity remains even when these effects are controlled for. Mefford suggests that this effect may be due to an improved labor relations climate or improved labor quality. Mefford's conclusions are specific to one labor-intensive consumer goods industry and may not be generalized beyond.

Criticisms of studies finding a positive union productivity effect can be placed in three major categories. One type of criticism directly confronts the logical basis of the argument behind the union voice mechanism. This criticism makes the point that the institutional view of unionism lacks theoretical justification. A second type of criticism faults the model specification. Brown and Medoff recognize that their specification of the model may have problems, but they do not believe that these problems are so restrictive as to preclude the usefulness of the test. A third type of criticism presents contrary findings that cast doubt on the robustness of the positive union effect conclusion.

The positive-union-productivity-effect theory is vague on how unions work within the production process to achieve productivity gains. In fact, Turnbull argues that the theoretical convictions, rather than the data, must be substantiated or refuted before the analysis of unions and productivity can progress.[4] Lower quit rates and improved handling of grievances are reported to be part of the reason unions may have higher productivity. But, as Turnbull points out, a much more detailed analysis of industrial relations is needed to answer the question of union productivity effects.

Hirsch and Addison find little support for the Freeman-Medoff position and speculate that the observed positive effect may be attributable to a shock response by management to the union situation.[5] This would imply differing production functions between union and nonunion firms. Specifically, the difference would be a larger managerial input for the union firms, with this being a contributing factor in the higher productivity apparently found. But, as described later, the model does not include different production functions for union and nonunion firms.

Several problems are possible with the specification of the model used in the Harvard studies. First, excepting the Clark studies, all assume identical production functions between union and nonunion firms.

Second, the dependent variable used in several of the aforementioned studies (Brown and Medoff; Brown, Freeman, and Leonard; and Frantz) is derived from value added per worker. The use of value added brings with it the distinct possibility that the model captures a union price effect instead of an output (productivity) effect. Any study that employs value added instead of a physical measure of production must be viewed as suspect. In addition, the quality of other inputs (specifically managerial), as well as organizational factors, is not controlled for in most studies.[6]

Morgan O. Reynolds has pointed out an additional problem in the model specification.[7] Reynolds argues that reliance on the explicit production function approach initiated by Brown and Medoff contains a flaw "that renders econometric estimates based on it incapable of resolving the question of what impact unions may have on productivity" (p. 443). He points out that if firms maximize profits, and trade unions impose higher-than-competitive wage rates on unionized firms, then the marginal productivity of unionized labor is necessarily greater than that of nonunion labor. Even if statistical controls for the quality of workers and capital/labor ratios are employed, "the firms burdened by union pricing must have higher marginal labor products because managers employ smaller amounts of labor than the nonunion firms that enjoy lower labor prices" (p. 444). Reynolds points out that using the Harvard model there is no way to discover the independent impact of unionization on productivity because there is no way to statistically separate observed marginal productivity differentials from union/nonunion price differentials. He concludes that unionization simply diverts employment from high-productivity sectors to low-productivity sectors and the observed union/nonunion productivity differential is simply a distortion in the allocation of scarce labor and capital induced by monopoly prices.

Yet another problem in the model specification has been identified by Lovell, Sickles, and Warren.[8] The authors point out that to derive a linear estimating equation, Brown and Medoff and others transformed an "intrinsically nonlinear" explanatory variable via a first-order Taylor-series approximation. The authors point out that the use of this approximation introduces a bias that necessarily results in an overstatement of the absolute value of the true union productivity effect.

In addition to the criticism of the model specification are several studies find evidence contrary to (or at least nonsupportive of) the positive union effect on productivity. These include studies by Pencavel, Clark, Warren, Bemmels, Boal, and Mitchell and Stone.[9] Pencavel studied the union effect on the production of the British coal-mining industry from 1900 to 1913. He determined that unions reduced coal output by 2.3 to 3.1 percent during this period. One of the appealing attributes of this study is that there was no union wage effect, and therefore the previously mentioned concern about mistaking the price effect for the output effect is mitigated.

Warren, in a time series study of private domestic business from 1948 to 1973, found a negative effect of unionization on productivity. Clark, in an analysis of product-line businesses of North American manufacturers, found a negative 2 to 3 percent union effect on productivity. Bemmels's analysis of 46 manufacturing plants in 1982 also indicates a negative union impact on productivity. He finds evidence that unions reduce the effectiveness of some managerial practices designed to increase productivity and that a poor labor management relations climate also reduces productivity.

Boal looked at the effect of unionism on productivity in 83 West Virginia coal mines in the early 1920s. His results indicate that unionism reduced productivity at small mines, but not at large mines. Mitchell and Stone's analysis of western U.S. sawmills permitted them to control for output quality and input usage. They found that unionized sawmills were between 12 and 21 percent less productive than nonunionized mills in 1986. They also found that when controls for product quality and raw material usage were not included, the estimate of union productivity was biased upward.

In addition to articles analyzing the union effect on the level of productivity, several analyze the effect unions have on total factor productivity growth. Some of these studies are by Mansfield, Link, Sveikauskas and Sveikauskas, Kendrick, Maki, and Hirsch and Link.[10] All of these studies found that unions have a negative effect on total factor productivity growth. In the case of the Sveikauskas-Sveikauskas study, the effect was statistically insignificant. In the other five studies, the effect was statistically significant. These studies provide a good deal of support for the hypothesis that unions hamper total factor productivity growth. But, as pointed out by Maki and by Hirsch and Link, this finding may not preclude a positive union effect on the level of productivity. A possible scenario would be a one-time positive union effect followed by slower productivity growth thereafter.

The findings concerning total factor productivity growth as well as the papers criticizing the Harvard studies cast considerable doubt on the robustness and generality of studies finding a positive union productivity effect. New studies on this issue continue to be published on a regular basis in various economic journals. The debate is not over, and from the available evidence in the economic literature, no one can say whether unions improve or hinder productivity. However, the idea of a positive union productivity effect is in definite retreat.

Having admitted that economists do not know with an overwhelming degree of certainty whether unions have a negative effect on productivity, can anything at all be said on this subject? Proponents of a positive union productivity effect have advanced the theory that unions may affect productivity through two general mechanisms: a shock mechanism and/or a collective voice mechanism. One aspect of collective voice is cooperation, and, while the literature on unions and productivity has not specifically analyzed unions, cooperation, and productivity, evidence on this subject does exist. Two separate areas must be investigated: evidence on unions and cooperation, and evidence on cooperation and productivity. Looking at the results of these two sets of literature and then combining them, we can come up with a partial answer to the question of what effect unions have on productivity.

UNIONS AND COOPERATION

This section looks at whether U.S. labor law, designed as it is to protect unions' rights to organize workers and bargain collectively, contributes to a poor industrial relations climate and thus inhibits labor-management cooperation. A good understanding of the National Labor Relations Act or Wagner Act is needed to evaluate the effect labor law has on the industrial relations climate and labor-management cooperation in the United States.

The National Labor Relations Act

The National Labor Relations Act (NLRA) or Wagner Act was passed in June 1935 to replace Section 7(a) of the National Industrial Recovery Act, which was declared unconstitutional in May 1935. For nearly two years after its passage, the NLRA did not exert much influence, but in 1937 the Supreme Court heard arguments in the Jones and Laughlin case and declared the NLRA constitutional. With this case, the court, by a broad interpretation of what affected commerce, greatly extended the power Congress wielded over commerce and laid the foundation for not only the NLRA but a general extension of the regulatory powers of the federal government as well. At least partly because of the NLRA and the

Jones and Laughlin case, union membership increased from 3.6 million in 1937 to 14 million in 1947, when the Taft-Hartley amendment to the NLRA was passed.

Why did Congress pass the NLRA? What reasons did proponents give for supporting the bill? The reasons seem to boil down to three: (1) it was hoped that the bill would reduce industrial strife; (2) it was hoped that the bill would give workers the opportunity to balance their collective bargaining power against the power of large employers and, through that power, obtain their just civil rights; and (3) it was hoped that the bill would promote a more equal distribution of income by transferring some of the income made by the capital owners to the workers. This increased purchasing power of the workers would help the country avoid in the future deep depressions such as the one that began in 1929. Inadequate purchasing power was seen by many as a direct cause of the Great Depression. Let us look at each of these reasons in a little more detail.

   1. Reduce industrial strife. The title of the bill as it moved through the Senate stated that it was a bill designed to "promote equality of bargaining power between employers and employees, to diminish the causes of labor disputes, to create a National Labor Relations Board and for other purposes." This title states a concept that many proponents of the bill held, namely, that the bill, if passed, would promote industrial peace. At the time the bill was being discussed, the country was in the midst of an intense era of industrial strife. Strikes had been occurring at record rates for at least two years, and many argued that most of the strikes were due to employers' failure to recognize the legitimate right of employees to bargain collectively. The NLRA was designed to ensure employees their rights to organize and join a union. In fact, the declaration of policy accompanying the bill states that it is meant not just to guarantee workers their right to bargain collectively but to encourage collective bargaining. Industrial strife, it was argued, would decline as employees and their unions would no longer have to fight and strike for recognition.

   2. Equalize bargaining power to promote workers' rights. Perhaps Senator Robert Wagner stated this argument most eloquently. He said:

   The national labor relations bill does not break with our traditions. It is the next step in the logical unfolding of man's eternal quest for freedom. For 25 centuries of recorded time before the

machine age we sought relief from nature's cruel and relentless
tyranny. Only 150 years ago did this country cast off the shack-
les of political despotism. And today, with economic problems
occupying the center of the stage, we strive to liberate the common man from destitution, from insecurity, and from human
exploitation. In this modern aspect of a time-worn problem the
isolated worker is a plaything of fate. Caught in the labyrinth of
modern industrialism and dwarfed by the size of corporate
enterprise, he can attain freedom and dignity only by cooperation with others of his group.[11]

In other words, Senator Wagner and many other proponents
believed that the only way workers could improve their conditions
was through the establishment of an organization big enough and
strong enough to successfully confront big businesses. The NLRA's
remedy for workers' ills was simply to fight perceived monopsony
power with monopoly power.

3. Increase workers' purchasing power. The Great Depression
had a profound influence on the last justification for the NLRA.
Many believed that a major cause of the depression was the
unequal distribution of income that had developed in the U.S.
economy and the resultant lack of purchasing power of the masses.
Many proponents argued that giant corporations had a vast capacity for production, but because the capital owners controlled so
much of the economy's wealth, not enough purchasing power existed to buy all the goods that could be produced. Thus, the economy
was subject to severe depressions.

Turning again to the NLRA's declaration of policy, we read,
"Experience has shown that in the absence of equality of bargaining
power the resultant failure to maintain equilibrium between the rate of
wages and the rate of industrial expansion impairs economic stability and
aggravates recurrent depressions, with consequent detriment to the general welfare and the free flow of commerce."[12]
To proponents of the NLRA, then, a more equal balancing of power
was essential. As stated by one proponent, "Unless we have, therefore,
collective bargaining, higher wages, and increased purchasing power, we
have got to take the other road of limited production." Limited production to this proponent meant collectivism or a planned economy.[13]
Of the three principal reasons given by proponents of the NLRA,
equalization of bargaining power was by far the most often cited. Based

on this, we must conclude that it was the main reason for the passage of the act.

The original NLRA contained only three basic techniques for achieving its objectives. First, the act prohibited employer conduct designed to interfere with workers' right to join a union. The nature of this conduct was spelled out in detail in five types of so-called unfair labor practices: (1) interference with, restraint of, or coercion of employees in union activities; (2) assisting or dominating a labor organization; (3) discriminating in employment for union membership or union activities, or lack of them; (4) discriminating for participation in National Labor Relations Board proceedings; (5) refusal to bargain collectively with a certified union.

Second, the act afforded industrial workers and unions a new method of organizing—the secret-ballot election.

Finally, the act established a quasi-judicial agency, the National Labor Relations Board (NLRB), whose function and duty were to enforce and administer the law, to listen to charges of unfair labor practices, to decide on those charges, and to administer the secret-ballot elections.

As stated by many proponents of the NLRA, it was designed not to dictate the particulars of collective bargaining or force, in any way, the employer to pay a certain wage or give certain benefits. As seen by proponents, the bill was simply a method of bringing workers to the bargaining table and ensuring their right to be there.

Opposition to the NLRA was intense in the business community, but that opposition did not translate into opposition in Congress, as the bill passed the Senate with a 63 to 12 vote, came out of the House Labor Committee with a unanimous recommendation, and passed the House on a voice vote (the opposition didn't even have enough strength to demand a different type of vote). Still, to understand the bill, we should note the various objections to it.

Perhaps the objection voiced most often by those few congressmen who did oppose the bill was its questionable constitutionality. This objection was also voiced by several business leaders, but they tended to emphasize other objections. The constitutionality of the NLRA, as we have already noted, was in question until the 1937 Jones and Laughlin case.

Another objection brought up by congressmen, employers, and even some employees was that the bill protected workers from coercion and intimidation by employers but said nothing about coercion and intimidation from unions or other employees. Several attempts were made to amend the bill to protect workers from union coercion. All were defeated. This issue resurfaced in later years and was dealt with in the 1947 Taft-Hartley amendment.

The bill proposed severe restrictions on company unions. This was another point of objection by many. Several employee groups, as well as many employers and a few congressmen, testified that many workers were happy with their company unions and did not want them outlawed. They believed that labor-management cooperation would suffer as a result of passage of the NLRA.

Another frequent, yet ignored, objection was that the act would not lead to industrial *peace* but would set the stage for unalterable antagonism and would lead to more industrial *strife*. Several congressmen predicted that the number of strikes would balloon after passage of the NLRA. Again, we see some indication that the potential negative effects of the bill on cooperation were noted and discussed.

Business leaders were concerned with the bill's effect on the potential monopoly power of unions. Several businesspersons noted that, by bestowing monopoly power on unions, the NLRA would cause costs to businesses to rise, and the public would end up paying for it. No congressmen voiced this opinion in the floor debates.

Two other objections to the bill that surfaced during testimony were concerns with closed shops (the bill actually changed nothing at all about the legality of closed shops) and the rights of employers (these were not mentioned at all in the bill).

The NLRA and Cooperation

Did the NLRA effectively cement an adversarial relationship between businesses and their employees that has stymied labor-management cooperative efforts as opponents thought it might? The potential for such an outcome definitely exists. As stated earlier, the purpose of the act was to fight monopsony with monopoly. The reasoning went like this: if large corporations have the power to trample on the rights of their employees, then we will set up an organization with equal power to force corporations to change their ways. This, in essence, is the adversarial model of industrial relations on which the NLRA was based. The model and the act require arm's-length collective bargaining and view cooperation between management and labor with suspicion—hence, the prohibition against company unions.

Let us look at the judicial history of the NLRA with regard to labor-management cooperative efforts to see if we can reasonably conclude that the adversarial assumptions of the law have inhibited labor-management cooperation.

We must first review two parts of the NLRA that are critical to our understanding of the judicial history of the act. The first is Section 2(5). This section defines a labor organization. It states that "the term 'labor organization' means any organization of any kind, or any agency or employee representation committee or plan, in which employees participate and which exists for the purpose, in whole or in part, of dealing with employers concerning grievances, labor disputes, wages, rates of pay, hours of employment, or conditions of work." The critical phrase in this section is "dealing with employers." According to the act, any group that is founded to deal with the employer on any condition of work is a labor organization and is covered by the act.

If an organization is covered by the act, then the second critical section of the act applies, namely Section 8(a)(2). This section states: "It shall be an unfair labor practice for an employer to dominate or interfere with the formation or administration of any labor organization or contribute financial or other support to it. Providing...an employer shall not be prohibited from permitting employees to confer with him during working hours without loss of time or pay." With regards to labor-management cooperation, the key word in this section is "dominate."   To show the importance of these two sections with regard to labor-management cooperation, we can outline a plausible scenario. Suppose an employer facing intense foreign competition wishes to improve efficiency through a form of employee participation. Management decides to form several ongoing committees that involve representatives of the workers to deal with such issues as employees' concerns, product quality, and productivity. Could an employer pursue this scheme and not be in violation of the NLRA?

We must first determine if our hypothetical employer's committees are labor organizations. In its 1959 *Cabot Carbon* decision, the Supreme Court made it clear that any organization that is concerned in any way with conditions of employment is a labor organization. The NLRB, in many cases, has reaffirmed this decision, most recently in its *Electromation* and *Dupont* decisions which we discuss in more detail later.

Since our employer's committees will discuss such things as employee concerns and productivity, these committees would be found to be labor organizations. In fact, the judicial history of the NLRA makes clear the fact that virtually all labor-management committees—whether they are quality circles, quality of work life programs, productivity committees, or whatever—are considered labor organizations under the law.[14]

Next, would our employer's committees be found to be in violation of Section 8(a)(2)? That is, would the NLRB and/or the courts rule that the committees are dominated by the employer? The Supreme Court has not issued a decision involving modern labor-management committees and Section 8(a)(2) of the NLRA, but the NLRB has. In the widely discussed *Electromation* case heard in 1991, an employer set up committees similar to those of our hypothetical employer. The NLRB ruled that the committees were labor organizations and were dominated or interfered with by the employer. The committees were in violation of Section 8(a)(2) because they were set up by the employer, their structures and functions were determined by the employer, they met on company time, and they received supplies from the employer. According to NLRB rulings, in this and other cases, an anti-union attitude or intent does not need to exist for a violation of Section 8(a)(2) to be found. Since it is our hypothetical employer's idea to establish the committees, and since the employer will decide what their agendas will be, it is obvious that the NLRB would find them to be a violation of the NLRA, even though they are a reaction not to a unionization drive but to foreign competition. As in the *Electromation* case, the NLRB would order the committees of our hypothetical employer to be disbanded.

Our hypothetical employer is a nonunion employer trying to deal with competition by improving efficiency. What would happen to a union employer that tried to set up similar committees? The NLRB recently heard just such a case. E. I. du Pont de Nemours and Company, a union company, established six safety committees and one fitness committee outside its collective bargaining commitments. The union filed an unfair labor practices suit claiming that the committees were labor organizations under Section 2(5) and were dominated by the firm in violation of Section 8(a)(2). In essence, the union alleged that the committees, which were modeled after DuPont's quality of work life committees, were a means for DuPont to bypass the union.

The NLRB sided with the union by finding that all of the committees were labor organizations and that all were dominated by the employer. In their ruling, the board members tried to emphasize that "there is some room for lawful cooperation under the Act." For instance, they noted that both brainstorming sessions and suggestion boxes are legal. They also noted that if a committee exists for the sole purpose of "imparting information" or for "planning education programs," then it would be legal.[15]

As in the *Electromation* case, the NLRB made clear in this case that if a committee or group is created by an employer, exists at the will of that employer, and deals, no matter how remotely, with any condition of employment, even if it is something like safety or fitness, it will be found to be in violation of the NLRA, and, if challenged, will be ordered disbanded. Our question is, What effective cooperative effort does not violate the NLRA? and here we emphasize *effective*.

The NLRA is based on the concept that labor and management are adversaries. All of their dealings must be at arm's length and must be channeled in such a way as to control the inherent conflict. Trying to make room in this legal environment for cooperative efforts is like trying to fit the proverbial square peg in a round hole.

After the recent rulings of the NLRB, little doubt can exist that U.S. labor laws, designed to promote unionization, are hostile to cooperation between management and labor. But before concluding that this legal environment has stifled productivity and thereby worsened the U.S. NAIRU, we must first ascertain if labor-management cooperation really improves productivity.

COOPERATION AND PRODUCTIVITY

Literature analyzing the effects of employee participation (or labor-management cooperation) on firm performance can be divided into three different categories. The first considers how employee participation in ownership or profits affects the performance of the firm. The second analyzes the impact employee participation in decision making has on firm performance. The third investigates the effects of programs that combine employee participation in ownership or profits with employee participation in decision making.

Employee Participation in Ownership or Profits

When we say employee participation in ownership or profits, what do we mean? Currently, many U.S. firms allow their employees to participate in ownership through employee stock ownership plans (ESOPs). The Employee Retirement Income Security Act of 1974 gave explicit encouragement to such plans, and many have been established since then. In addition, many firms have allowed employees to participate in profits via formal profit-sharing plans. These plans are of two types: "deferred" profit-sharing plans, which provide retirement benefits, and "cash" plans, which pay out profits to workers as they are earned. More than 90 percent of all profit-sharing plans are of the deferred type.

The literature on the impact of these types of plans is nothing if not mixed. Some studies find that ESOPs and profit sharing improve firm productivity; others find that they do not. On balance, the literature seems to indicate that neither an ESOP program nor a profit-sharing program, if enacted alone, will have much of a lasting positive influence on productivity.[16]

Employee Participation in Decision Making

What about employee participation in decision making? Here we refer to labor-management committees and teams, quality circles, and other methods of giving shop floor workers more say in decisions that have traditionally been made solely by management. These types of plans have been put in question by current labor laws.

As in the case of employee participation in ownership and profits, the literature on the impact on productivity of employee participation in decision making is mixed. Many studies have been published showing that such programs increase productivity. In addition, surveys of plant managers indicate that they see participation as an effective way to improve performance. But not all of the evidence is positive. A paper by Edwin Locke, David Schweiger, and Gary Latham that reviews 50 studies on participation shows that a majority of the studies find no significant impact of participation on productivity.[17] A similar conclusion was reached by John Wagner and Richard Gooding in their review of the literature.[18] We cannot definitely conclude from the literature that employee participation in decision making by itself will lead to higher productivity. Most of the literature seems to answer the question "Does employee participation lead to productivity growth?" with "It depends." It depends on many firm-specific, factors and few broad generalizations can be reached.

Employee Participation in Both

But what about when employee participation in decision making is combined with employee participation in profits? Many such programs are referred to as gainsharing plans. Do gainsharing plans typically result in increased productivity? The literature here gives a firm answer of yes. Organizations that give employees a say in managerial decisions and then reward good decisions (decisions that result in reduced labor costs, higher profits, and such) have higher productivity.[19]

In summary, the literature on employee participation basically comes to the conclusion that participation significantly increases productivity when that participation is multifaceted (i.e. when it involves both decision making and profit sharing), when it enjoys the support of many levels of an organizational hierarchy, and when it is made a permanent part of the culture of the firm.[20]

CONCLUSIONS AND RECOMMENDATIONS

Throughout the late 1970s and 1980s, interest in labor-management cooperation in the United States surged, as did actual cooperative experiments. Most analysts agree that this surge was primarily due to the difficult economic climate faced by U.S. firms. Increased competition, both domestic and foreign, required U.S. managers to consider new techniques and methodologies.

Our review of the literature on employee participation and firm performance has shown that turning to cooperation can be a fruitful endeavor. But we have also shown that U.S. labor law, at best, looks on labor-management cooperation with suspicion. In fact, current U.S. labor law has the potential to significantly slow, if not stop, the introduction of cooperative programs. Has this potential been realized? In other words, would productivity-enhancing, cooperative programs have been introduced sooner and spread further if labor law had been more accommodating? Our answer to this question must be yes—U.S. labor law has stymied productivity by limiting cooperative efforts.

In attacking this conclusion, some will undoubtedly point to the number of such programs in existence and their growth. Our response comes not from an empirical study showing what would have happened if labor law had been different but from a simple understanding of the growth process. Biological plants like alfalfa do not thrive in a harsh environment. A farmer who plants alfalfa in the middle of the summer in Arizona and waters it only once every two weeks cannot expect to have a good crop. A few of the alfalfa plants may actually survive, but most will not. The same is true of cooperative efforts in a climate that is hostile to such efforts. No matter how many seeds are planted, say, by the success of such programs in other countries or the quantity of papers published by experts, only a relatively few programs will survive and mature.

Interest in labor-management cooperation—thus, seeding—has been intense, but the hostile legal environment has prevented the United States from reaping a bounteous crop of productivity-enhancing programs. Because we have no way of knowing what our productivity growth would have been absent this legal environment, which is based on an adversarial model of industrial relations, we have no way of knowing what our unemployment would have been. But, given the evidence presented here, the proposition can be made that the U.S. unemployment rate will improve with a change in U.S. labor law. Stronger productivity growth means higher feasible real wages, and if target real wages do not surge ahead of feasible real wages, a lower unemployment rate will result. Such changes will lead to a more efficient economy with a lower NAIRU and higher human capital formation.

One aspect of labor-management cooperation that we have not mentioned is that it often results in workers' being more satisfied with their jobs. In other words, they achieve a greater degree of self-fulfillment. Virtually all human beings need to know that they are important, that what they do matters. Most want to be productive. Labor-management cooperation is a way to help workers satisfy these needs to the benefit of both workers and business firms and, ultimately, the entire economy.

What changes could we make to our labor laws to improve the situation? Two changes are possible and perhaps desirable. The first is to simply repeal Section 8(a)(2) of the NLRA. This has been advocated by many labor law experts, including a few who want more protections for labor unions.[21] Repealing section 8(a)(2) would mean that even if labor-management committees, quality circles, and other cooperative programs were found to be labor organizations under Section 2(5), they could not be disbanded unless they were used as a weapon against union organizing or collective bargaining efforts, in which case other sections of the NLRA and other labor laws would apply. Repeal of Section 8(a)(2) would not give employers an incentive to install cooperative programs; it would simply remove the current disincentive. Labor law would then be neutral on the issue of cooperation.

The other change that could be made to labor law is to move from neutrality on cooperation to promotion. This book has consistently emphasized that increased costs to business result in a higher NAIRU. Most government regulations result in increased costs. While not advocating a government-regulated or mandated program of cooperation, we do suggest that gain sharing be encouraged. A simple way to encourage gain sharing would be to allow firms that institute a genuine gain-sharing program, including both employee participation in decision making and employee participation in economic rewards, to pay a lower tax rate.

NOTES

1. Charles Brown and James Medoff, "Trade Unions in the Production Process," *Journal of Political Economy* 86 (June 1978), pp. 355-78.

2. J. R. Frantz, "The Impact of Trade Unions on Production in The Wooden Household Furniture Industry," senior honors thesis, Harvard University, Cambridge, MA, March 1976; Brown and Medoff, "Trade Unions in the Production Process"; Kim Clark, "The Impact of Unionization on Productivity: A Case Study," *Industrial and Labor Relations Review* 33 (July 1980a), pp. 451-69; Kim B. Clark, "Unionization and Productivity: Micro-Econometric Evidence," *Quarterly Journal of Economics* 95 (December 1980b), pp. 613-39; Richard B. Freeman and James L. Medoff, *What Do Unions Do?* (New York: Basic Books, 1984); M. Connerton, Richard B. Freeman, and James L. Medoff, "Productivity and Industrial Relations: The Case of U.S. Bituminous Coal," mimeographed, Harvard University, Cambridge, MA, 1983; and Steven Allen, "Unionized Construction Workers Are More Productive," *Quarterly Journal of Economics* 99 (May 1984), pp. 249-74.

3. Steven G. Allen, "The Effect of Unionism on Productivity in Privately and Publicly Owned Hospitals and Nursing Homes," *Journal of Labor Research* 7 (Winter 1986), pp. 59-68; Robert N. Mefford, "The Effect of Unions on Productivity in a Multinational Manufacturing Firm," *Industrial and Labor Relations Review* 40 (October 1986), pp. 105-14.

4. Peter J. Turnbull, "Trade Unions and Productivity: Opening the Harvard Black Boxes," *Journal of Labor Research* 12 (Spring 1991), pp. 135-50.

5. Barry T. Hirsch and John T. Addison, *The Economic Analysis of Unions: New Approaches and Evidence* (Winchester, MA: Allen and Unwin, 1986), pp. 192-208; see also John T. Addison and Barry T. Hirsch, "Unions Effects on Productivity, Profits, and Growth: Has the Long Run Arrived?" *Journal of Labor Economics* 7 (January 1989), pp. 72-105.

6. For a fuller treatment of these arguments, see John T. Addison, "Are Unions Good for Productivity?" *Journal of Labor Research* 3 (Spring 1982), pp. 125-38; John T. Addison and A. H. Barnett, "The Impact of Unions on Productivity," *British Journal of Industrial Relations* 20 (July 1982), pp. 145-62; John T. Addison, "What Do Unions Really Do?" *Journal of Labor Research* 4 (Spring 1985), pp. 127-46; and Hirsch and Addison, *The Economic Analysis of Unions*, pp. 192-208.

7. Morgan O. Reynolds, "Trade Unions in the Production Process Reconsidered," *Journal of Political Economy* 94 (April 1986), pp. 443-447.

8. C. A. Knox Lovell, Robin C. Sickles, and Ronald S. Warren, Jr., "The Effect of Unionization on Labor Productivity: Some Additional Evidence," *Journal of Labor Research* 9 (Winter 1988), pp. 55-63.

9. John J. Pencavel, "The Distributional and Efficiency Effects of Trade

Unions in Britain," *British Journal of Industrial Relations* 15 (July 1977), pp. 137-56; Kim B. Clark, "Unionization and Firm Performance: The Impact on Profits, Growth, and Productivity," *American Economic Review* 74 (July 1984), pp. 893-919; Ronald S. Warren, Jr., "The Effect of Unionization on Labor Productivity: Some Time-Series Evidence," *Journal of Labor Research* 6 (Spring 1985), pp. 199-208; Brian Bemmels, "How Unions Affect Productivity in Manufacturing Plants," *Industrial and Labor Relations Review* 40 (January 1987), pp. 241 - 253; William M. Boal, "Unionism and Productivity in West Virginia Coal Mining," *Industrial and Labor Relations Review* 43 (April 1990), pp. 390-405; Merwin W. Mitchell and Joe A. Stone, "Union Effects on Productivity: Evidence from Western U.S. Sawmills," *Industrial and Labor Relations Review* 46 (October 1992), pp. 135-145.

10. Edwin Mansfield, "Basic Research and Productivity Increase in Manufacturing," *American Economic Review* 70 (December 1980), pp. 863-73; Albert N. Link, "Basic Research and Productivity Increase in Manufacturing: Additional Evidence," *American Economic Review* 71 (December 1981), pp. 1111-12; Catherine Defina Sveikauskas and Leo Sveikauskas, "Industry Characteristics and Productivity Growth," *Southern Economic Journal* 48 (January 1982), pp. 769-74; John Kendrick, *Interindustry Differences in Productivity Growth* (Washington, DC: American Enterprise Institute, 1983); Dennis R. Maki, "The Effects of Unions and Strikes on the Rate of Growth of Total Factor Productivity in Canada," *Applied Economics* 15 (1983), pp. 29-41; and Barry T. Hirsch and Albert N. Link, "Unions, Productivity and Productivity Growth," *Journal of Labor Research* 5 (Winter 1984), pp. 29-37.

11. *Congressional Record*, 74th Congress (Washington, DC: Government Printing Office), p. 7565.

12. Senate Committee on Education and Labor, March 11, 1935, p. 1.

13. "Testimony of Charlton Ogburn, AFL Council, before the Senate Committee on Education and Labor," March 11, 1935.

14. Shaun G. Clark, "Rethinking the Adversarial Model in Labor Relations: An Argument for Repeal of Section 8 (a)(2)," *Yale Law Journal* 96 (July 1987), pp. 2021-50.

15. Case 25-CA-19818, United States of America, before the National Labor Relations Board: Electromation, Inc. and International Brotherhood of Teamsters, Local Union No. 1049, AFL-CIO and "Action Committees," 309 NLRB No. 163.

16. Raymond Russell, "Forms and Extent of Employee Participation in the Contemporary United States," *Work and Occupations* 15 (November 1988), pp. 374-95, gives a review of the literature.

17. Edwin A. Locke, David M. Schweiger, and Gary P. Latham, "Participation in Decision Making: When Should It Be Used?" *Organizational Dynamics* (Winter 1986), pp. 65-79.

18. John A. Wagner and Richard Gooding, "Shared Influence and Organization Behavior: A Meta-Analysis of Situational Variables Expected to Moderate Participation-Outcome Relationships," *Academy of Management Journal* 30 (September 1987), pp. 524-41.

19. Russell, "Forms and Extent of Employee Participation"; and George T. Milkovich, "Gain Sharing and Profit Sharing as Strategic Considerations," in Myron J. Roomkin (ed.), *Profit Sharing and Gain Sharing* (Metuchen, NJ: IMLR Press, 1990), pp. 109-22.

20. Ibid.

21. For example, Clarke, "Rethinking the Adversarial Model in Labor Relations"; Raymond L. Hogler and Guillermo Grenrer, *Employee Participation and Labor Law in the American Workplace* (New York: Quorum Books, 1992).

CHAPTER 8

PRODUCTIVITY
AND THE NAIRU

C hapter 6 introduced a very important topic—productivity and the NAIRU. This topic was examined within the context of a discussion of unions and labor law. This chapter pursues this issue of productivity and the NAIRU somewhat further, beginning with a brief review of how a change in productivity growth can affect the NAIRU.

As discussed in Chapter 2, at any given time there is a limit to the real wages that an economy can afford to pay its workers; in other words, there is a "feasible real wage." The level and rate of growth of feasible real wages depend on the level and rate of growth of productivity. A man cannot run faster than his legs will carry him, and an economy cannot pay *real* wages in excess of the underlying productive capacity of the economy. A slowdown in the rate of growth of productivity in the economy means that, other things being equal, the rate of growth of aggregate feasible real wages also slows down. If workers do not recognize this slowdown and they continue to demand real wage increases that are in excess of feasible real wages, inflationary pressure will result and unemployment will increase. The resulting unemployment impacts marginal workers the hardest. In essence, what happens is that protected workers (members of government bureaucracies, union workers, and others) win at the expense of nonprotected workers.

THE RELATIONSHIP BETWEEN PRODUCTIVITY
GROWTH AND THE NAIRU

What has happened to U.S. productivity growth and unemployment during the past few decades? Figure 8.1 shows the 10-year moving average of annual unemployment rates discussed in Chapter 2 and a 5-year moving average of productivity (output per hour of all persons in the nonfarm business sector). Of particular interest is the period from the mid-1970s to the early 1980s, when the U.S. unemployment rate increased dramatically. What was happening to productivity growth during this period? As the figure shows, productivity growth was slowing in this period. Experts in the analysis of productivity growth, for example, John Kendrick, Elliot Grossman, and Edward Denison, have clearly identified the beginning of this slowdown in the United States as the period 1966-67, with the slowdown becoming more acute after 1973.[1] As pointed out by Michael Bruno and Jeffrey Sachs, aggregate GDP per person employed grew at an average annual rate of 2.7 percent in the period from 1960 to 1967. It slowed to 1.6 percent in the period from 1967 to 1973 and only 0.2 percent in the period from 1973 to 1980.[2] In other words, U.S. productivity growth slowed, and the U.S. unemployment rate increased at just about the same time. Did the slowdown in productivity growth cause the increase in the unemployment rate?

FIGURE 8.1

TEN-YEAR MOVING AVERAGE OF U.S. ANNUAL UNEMPLOYMENT RATES AND PRODUCTIVITY CHANGE*

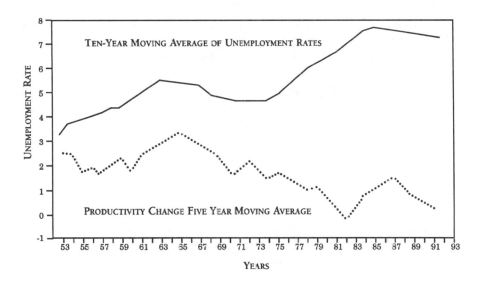

*Source: U.S. Department of Labor, Bureau of Labor Statistics, *Monthly Labor Review*, various issues.

Economic theory clearly predicts that a slowdown in the growth of productivity may cause a reduction in feasible real wages and thus may cause the NAIRU to increase. Yet, the case linking the slowdown in productivity growth to the increase in unemployment is not clear-cut. Before we can reasonably argue that the slowdown in productivity growth contributed to an increase in the U.S. NAIRU, two important questions must be answered. First, what is the direction of causation? Did the productivity slowdown cause unemployment to increase, or did an increase in unemployment cause productivity growth to slow? Second, did one or more outside factors cause both productivity growth to fall and unemployment to increase at the same time so that no causal relationship between productivity growth and the NAIRU exists?

Direction of Causation

George Johnson and Richard Layard have argued for causation running from the slowdown in productivity growth to an increase in unemployment.[3] They point out that productivity growth fell in virtually all industrialized countries in the early 1970s, and the unemployment rate also increased in these same countries. But Layard points out that the fall in productivity growth should have affected the unemployment rate only until workers accepted reality and did not push for real wage increases above what the reduced level of productivity growth could support.[4] Many years have passed since productivity growth slowed, and workers should have adapted by now. In Layard's view, a failure to adapt to a slower rate of productivity growth cannot explain the present NAIRU.

Bruno and Sachs also point out that the fall in the growth of productivity and the increase in unemployment have been common across almost all industrialized countries. But they argue that causation may run from unemployment to productivity growth. They point out that whatever the cause of high unemployment, it is plausible that it has had a profound effect on productivity by (1) slowing the sectoral reallocation of labor from low- to high-productivity sectors; (2) stifling gains that resulted from economies of scale in production and distribution; (3) reducing the within-firm upgrading of labor that occurs in a high-employment economy; and (4) inducing labor hoarding in many firms, in some cases for several years.[5]

At first glance, both arguments seem reasonable. Slower productivity growth could have contributed to an increase in unemployment, or high unemployment could have reduced productivity. To confuse matters even more, there is the possibility that no causal relationship existed between productivity and unemployment in the early 1970s to early 1980s period, and one or more other factors could have caused productivity growth to fall and unemployment to rise at the same time.

Factors Affecting Both Productivity and Unemployment

What factors could have played such a role? The literature on the decline in productivity growth cites several factors that may have played a role in its decline and at the same time affected the NAIRU.

Capital formation is an oft-discussed factor in the productivity literature. The argument is that capital formation lagged, causing the capital/labor ratio to tail off and productivity growth to slow. We will not analyze the basis of this argument. Our analysis is interested only in finding out if a slowdown in capital formation could have independently caused both a slowdown in productivity growth and an increase in unemployment. If such a slowdown in capital formation did occur, it may have affected productivity growth. What about the NAIRU?

Within our framework, the NAIRU increases with an imbalance between feasible real wages and the real wages that workers demand and obtain. The capital formation rate is unlikely to affect the real wage that workers demand independent of its impact on productivity, and the capital formation rate can affect the feasible real wage only through its impact on productivity. Therefore, it probably cannot be a factor that independently affected both productivity and unemployment.

What about research and development (R & D) spending? Several analysts have identified R & D spending as a contributor to the decline in productivity growth. Could it also have affected the NAIRU? As in the case of capital formation, R & D spending could have reduced the feasible real wage, but only through its impact on productivity. R & D spending is not likely to have affected the real wage that workers demanded.

What about the increase in energy prices, specifically, the 1973 oil shock? At first glance, this factor looks promising simply because of timing. Although productivity growth had begun to slow in the United States by about 1967, it slowed significantly more after 1973, and the NAIRU increased after 1973. Could a significant increase in oil prices have contributed to the decline in the rate of productivity growth? Several analysts have argued yes. They point out that when the relative price of an input rises, output per unit of other input factors (such as labor and capital) must fall. Profit will also fall, and the profit squeeze will cause an investment slowdown, which, in turn, affects the accumulation of capital, thereby contributing to a slowdown in labor productivity.[6] In other words, a significant increase in oil prices could have contributed to a slowdown in productivity growth. In a previous chapter, we outlined how a price shock can increase the NAIRU. In other words, the oil price shock is one factor that could have caused some movement in both productivity growth and the NAIRU.

Another factor identified in the literature as a potential cause of the productivity slowdown is government regulations. Regulations may slow the growth of productivity by increasing business costs without increasing output. Excessive regulations may also discourage productivity by affecting the business climate, increasing uncertainty with its accompanying effects on planning and investment. Government regulations definitely have the potential to reduce productivity, and several researchers have argued that government regulations did, in fact, play a significant role in the productivity growth slowdown. Could regulations also have played a part in the increase in the NAIRU? The analysis in Chapter 4 leads us to answer yes.

Two other factors that some analysts argue may have affected productivity growth are demographic changes in the labor force and structural changes in the economy. As explained previously, by structural changes the analysts mean shifts in the composition of aggregate output between industries, such as the shift of employees from manufacturing industries to service industries. Demographic changes could affect productivity growth if less productive *workers* increase proportionally in the labor force. Similarly, structural changes could affect productivity growth if less productive *industries* increase proportionally in the economy.

As already noted, one explanation for an increase in the NAIRU is increasing mismatch between available jobs and workers prepared to take those jobs. Mismatch can be caused or exacerbated by demographic changes and/or economic structural changes. Thus, these two factors are also *potential* causes of both the decline in the rate of productivity growth and the increase in the U.S. NAIRU. But, as pointed out in previous chapters, these two factors may not have had much to do with the increase in the U.S. NAIRU in *practice*.

CONCLUSIONS AND RECOMMENDATIONS

What can we say to this point about productivity growth and unemployment? First, economists have reached no consensus on whether the primary direction of causation runs from productivity growth to unemployment or from unemployment to productivity growth. A correlation between the two obviously existed from the early 1970s to the early 1980s. This correlation may have been the result of a causal relationship between the two, or it may have been the result of other factors influencing both. For instance, our brief review reveals that price shocks, like the 1973-74 oil price shock, may have affected both. Changes in government regulations may have had a similar effect. Structural and/or demographic changes may also have affected both productivity growth and unemployment.

One thing is clear: several things can be done that will improve U.S. productivity growth, like reducing the burden of government regulations and decreasing labor mismatch. If these things do increase productivity growth, they will also have a beneficial impact on the NAIRU. We must also keep in mind that increases in our standard of living depend to a large extent on the rate of our productivity growth. If policies exist that will both improve productivity growth and decrease unemployment, a double incentive exists to implement them.

While no consensus has yet been reached on the causes of the productivity slowdown, for policy recommendation purposes, such a consensus is not necessary. As long as identification of factors that will effectively improve productivity growth is possible, a set of policy tools can be prescribed to increase feasible real wage growth and attack the high NAIRU problem through increases in feasible real wages. Up to this point, several policies whose primary purpose is to reduce the NAIRU, not to improve productivity growth, have been discussed. Implementation of several of these policies may also result in increased productivity growth. What are these policies?

Chapter 3 discussed mismatch unemployment. As just mentioned, structural and/or demographic factors have not only been linked to increased unemployment but have also been linked by some analysts to the productivity growth slowdown. If structural change did, indeed, contribute to the productivity growth slowdown, then any policy recommendations made in this area to combat unemployment should also have a positive spillover effect on productivity growth.

One major recommendation concerning mismatch unemployment is to build a world-class education system. This is one of the most important things we can do to improve average productivity in the United States. Clearly, better-educated and better-trained employees are more productive employees. Education reform thus comes doubly recommended.

Chapter 4 discussed government regulations. As just mentioned, some analysts link increased government regulations to reduced productivity growth. At first glance, it would seem obvious that government regulations reduce productivity growth because they increase costs. In other words, they increase the number of person-hours needed to produce any given level of output. Remember that productivity is usually measured as output per person-hour. This simple explanation may not be totally accurate. Some analysts have argued that government regulations actually increase output, but perhaps not the type of output that shows up in productivity numbers. For instance, the resulting cleaner air or safer workplaces can, in a sense, be considered outputs. Do regulations add enough to output, whether measured or not, to justify their costs? This leads us to propose that cost-benefit calculations be conducted for all government regulations. We need to know if the output gains due to government regulations are worth their costs. The recommendations in Chapter 4 on government regulations should help to illuminate and limit the negative effects that government regulations can have on productivity growth.

Chapter 5 contained several recommendations regarding social welfare. Would these recommendations perhaps also help improve productivity growth? Some of the recommendations on reforming the unemployment insurance system dealt with the training, retraining, and basic education of unemployed workers. If the implementation of these recommendations resulted in better-educated and better-trained workers, then they would result in better U.S. productivity growth. The same can be said of the recommendations on welfare reform. If the welfare system could be reformed so as to put better-educated people into the workforce, then productivity, on average, would improve. Again, social welfare reform comes doubly recommended as a tool to reduce unemployment.

This book has also made a policy recommendation concerning labor unions—repeal Section 8(a)(2) of the NLRA, which currently prohibits many types of labor-management cooperation. This policy, if implemented, would likely result in improved productivity growth. As reviewed previously, the effect of unions on productivity growth is unclear, but the effect of a good cooperative system is not. Cooperation coupled with a sharing of rewards has been shown to improve productivity. One of the main reasons to reform our labor laws is the promised rewards in the area of productivity growth and thus the promised improvement in our unemployment rate. The same argument applies to the recommendations concerning gain-sharing systems.

In summary, virtually all of the policy recommendations this book has made thus far to reduce the U.S. unemployment rate can be doubly recommended because they have the potential to improve U.S. productivity growth.

Before concluding this chapter, it is worth noting that some economists already see evidence that increasing productivity growth in the late 1980s and early 1990s has reduced the U.S. NAIRU. Robert Gordon, for one, has recently suggested that increasing productivity has helped reduce the NAIRU from 6 to 5.5 percent. Many businesspeople support this viewpoint. Other economists are not yet ready to say that productivity growth has increased enough to reduce the NAIRU significantly.[7] Whether increasing productivity has or has not already reduced the NAIRU, we can be optimistic that if productivity growth continues to increase the NAIRU will come down.

NOTES

1. John W. Kendrick and Elliot S. Grossman, *Productivity: The United States' Trends and Cycles* (Baltimore: Johns Hopkins University Press, 1980); Edward F. Denison, "Explanations of Declining Productivity Growth," *Survey of Current Business*, August 1979, pp. 1-24.

2. Michael Bruno and Jeffrey D. Sachs, *Economics of Worldwide Stagflation* (Cambridge: Harvard University Press, 1985), p. 249.

3. George E. Johnson and Richard Layard, "The Natural Rate of Unemployment: Explanation and Policy," in O. Ashenfelter and R. Layard (eds.), *Handbook of Labor Economics, Volume 2* (New York: Elsevier Science, 1986), Chapter 16.

4. Richard Layard, *How to Beat Unemployment* (Oxford, England: Oxford University Press, 1986).

5. Bruno and Sachs, *Economics of Worldwide Stagflation.*

6. Ibid., p. 249.

7. Amanda Bennett, "Business and Academia Clash over a Concept: 'Natural' Jobless Rate," *Wall Street Journal*, January 24, 1995, p. 1.

CHAPTER 9

SUMMARY

T his final chapter will briefly review the arguments presented in earlier chapters. The purpose is to draw in all of the loose ends and
complete a picture of what the United States can do to reduce the
unemployment rate that is compatible with stable inflation.

THE COSTS OF UNEMPLOYMENT

Chapter 1 outlined some of the costs associated with unemployment.
It noted that, in monetary terms, an unemployment rate of 7 percent costs
the United States at least $400 billion in lost output. This lost output does
not begin to add up the total cost of unemployment. In terms of social
and human costs, unemployment has been linked to alcoholism, child
abuse, family breakdown, vandalism and criminal behavior, psychiatric
hospitalizations, suicide, homicide, and other problems.

Unemployment is not an insignificant problem in the United States.
Currently, the United States is unable to drop its unemployment rate
much below the 6 percent for any length of time before inflation begins
to accelerate. In other words, the United States' nonaccelerating inflation
rate of unemployment or the rate of unemployment that is consistent
with stable inflation is currently about 6 percent. At present, the U.S.
economy must keep more than 7 million people unemployed just to keep
inflation from accelerating.

If unemployment is so expensive, why not allow inflation to rise and
do whatever is necessary to force the unemployment rate down? The reason is that continuously accelerating inflation would result. Continuously
accelerating inflation would damage the economy so severely that it
might eventually collapse. Even if it did not collapse, our experience with
unemployment and inflation in the 1970s has taught us that, except in

the very short run, a little more inflation cannot be traded for a little less unemployment. Eventually, the economy ends up with more of both. In addition, a well-functioning price mechanism forms the basis of any market-based economy. We cannot afford to undermine that basis. Finally, the financial markets will not allow us to pursue a high inflation policy. If we attempted to do so, exchange rates would dive and the markets would force up interest rates, slowing the economy and pushing the unemployment rate higher.

Must we just live with a minimum unemployment rate of 6-7 percent? No! We can lower the unemployment rate that is consistent with stable inflation. That is what this book is all about. What have we discovered thus far?

MISMATCH UNEMPLOYMENT

In Chapter 3, we discussed the jobs summit held in Detroit, Michigan, in March 1994. Invited to this summit were the finance, labor, commerce, and economics ministers of the G-7 nations (Britain, Canada, France, Germany, Italy, Japan, and the United States). The attendees met to discuss the severe and continuing unemployment problems of their countries and to come up with a list of policies to combat unemployment. Central to the discussions of the ministers was the issue of mismatch unemployment. Perhaps the main theme of the summit was that if we simply train our workers better in order to combat mismatch unemployment, we will reduce our unemployment rate significantly. Is this a correct diagnosis of our current unemployment problems? In Chapter 3, several factors were identified that may have caused mismatch unemployment to rise. First, demographic changes were examined. Note was made of the fact that while some economists argue that demographic changes probably caused a slight increase in unemployment, others argue that it did not. Taken as a whole, a conservative assessment of the literature would be that, at most, demographic changes in the labor force played a minor role in the increase in the unemployment rate. We must look elsewhere to find the major cause or causes.

Another factor discussed in Chapter 3 that may have caused mismatch unemployment to rise is an increase in regional unemployment. Some analysts have pointed to industrial shifts from the Rust Belt to the Sun Belt as a major cause of the increasing unemployment rate. But changes in the difference between unemployment rates in Rust Belt versus Sun Belt states do not fit a pattern of increasing regional mismatch. In addition, data on U.S. mobility seem to indicate that workers have adjusted to regional disparities in employment and unemployment by moving.

Finally, skill mismatch was examined as a factor that may have increased the NAIRU. Skill mismatch may have resulted from such changes in the industrial structure as the change from an economy based on agriculture to one based on manufacturing and then on services or from an increase in the technical skill requirements of today's jobs.

Our review of the literature indicated that skill mismatch is a popular notion, but it is backed up by little hard empirical evidence. Few studies have found a statistically significant skill-mismatch effect, even for European countries where mismatch unemployment is thought to be a bigger problem than in the United States. An increase in skill mismatch as a factor causing the NAIRU to increase cannot be totally ruled out, nor can it be confirmed.

To fight skill mismatch, some have recommended government-sponsored training programs. Others have recommended regulations requiring firms to spend a certain percentage of their revenue on training and retraining or face harsh penalties. Evidence indicates that firms are willing to train workers in the specific skills they require. What firms want and the United States needs are educated, *trainable* workers. Education reform is, therefore, what the United States needs to combat what structural unemployment exists. Let the United States build the best education system in the world, and we will have few skill-mismatch unemployment problems. An integral part of building this world-class education system must be competition between providers—in other words, choice.

In summary, Chapter 3 argued that the diagnosis of the U.S. unemployment problems given at the jobs summit is probably not correct. At most, mismatch unemployment is responsible for only a small part of our high unemployment rate, and extensive training programs will not appreciably lower our unemployment rate. Such programs, although perhaps politically expedient, will be very expensive and will further weaken the public's already shaken confidence in our government.

GOVERNMENT REGULATION

Chapter 4 noted that shocks to business costs, such as might have been caused by the 1973-74 and 1979 oil price increases, can increase the unemployment rate by creating inflationary pressure. We discussed several types of business costs that may have increased and caused unemployment to increase, but we ended up focusing on increased costs due to government regulation.

Although the numbers on the costs of government regulation do not inspire a great deal of confidence, the costs of government regulation have undoubtedly increased significantly since 1960 and have probably contributed to a nontrivial increase in business costs and thus an increase in the U.S. NAIRU. At a minimum, federal regulation now costs $580 billion annually. State and local regulations may add a like amount to regulation costs. For many firms, the government-imposed costs are so important that they will not add workers to their payroll unless they simply have no other choice. Anecdotal evidence, if not empirical evidence, definitely indicates that government regulation costs contribute to unemployment.

What can be done to counter this negative influence of regulation costs on inflation and the NAIRU? Chapter 4 briefly discussed a bill introduced in the Senate by Orrin Hatch that would require that before new regulations are enacted, a thorough cost-benefit analysis be conducted. The analysis would include a consideration of alternatives and an analysis of all compliance costs. In addition, the bill, if enacted, would require that the least expensive alternative be implemented and, for the first three years that the regulation is in place, its costs would have to be offset by revocation or revision of existing regulations. This book strongly recommends that this bill or one like it be quickly enacted. We are only just beginning to understand how extensive and how damaging government regulation is. Few economists have formally linked regulation costs to increase in the NAIRU, but the United States cannot afford to ignore this issue any longer.

UNEMPLOYMENT INSURANCE AND SOCIAL WELFARE

Chapter 5 turned our discussion to the relationship between the NAIRU and programs like unemployment insurance and other social welfare programs. Increases in the payments of such programs that are directed toward working-age individuals will increase the reservation wage of the unemployed, meaning that they will be more choosy about the jobs they will consider and will choose to be unemployed for longer periods of time. In addition, some people will opt out of the labor force who would otherwise be in the labor force. In general, increases in social welfare transfers will reduce the effectiveness of any given level of unemployment at controlling inflation. Thus, a higher level of unemployment will be required to ensure stable or nonaccelerating inflation.

As reviewed in Chapter 5, social welfare payments have increased dramatically in the United States. The total of all social welfare expenditures increased from about 13 percent of personal income in 1960 to about 23 percent in 1976 and has remained at about that level to the present. Even after subtracting out Social Security and education payments, social welfare expenditures still nearly doubled as a percentage of personal income between 1960 and 1976, increasing from about 6 percent to nearly 12 percent.

The increase in U.S. social welfare expenditures, combined with the fact that the U.S. NAIRU was increasing at virtually the same time, at least suggests that increases in social welfare expenditures may have contributed to an increase in the NAIRU. If we look beyond the United States to the European experience with social welfare payments and unemployment, there can be little doubt that increasing social welfare payments has the potential to significantly increase the NAIRU. Evidence was cited in Chapter 5 documenting the much worse unemployment experience Europe has had when compared with the United States. To review, the unemployment rate in the European Community averaged nearly 10 percent during the 1982-92 decade, and even during the peak years in economic activity the rate was still more than 9 percent. In addition, much of Europe's unemployment was long-term in nature. According to David Henderson in 1989, only 1.2 percent of the U.S. labor force was unemployed for longer than 13 weeks; the comparable rates for European countries were four to seven times as high. In the United States, the number of people unemployed for 12 months or more was less than 6 percent of the total number of unemployed. In Europe, the numbers ranged from a low of 49 percent for Germany to a high of 72 percent for Italy.[1]

Many analysts attribute Europe's much worse unemployment experience to the fact that it subsidizes unemployment so heavily.[2] As noted in Chapter 5, European countries pay their unemployed workers a higher proportion of previous take-home pay and do so for a much longer period of time than does the United States. In addition, countries in Europe have regulated the hiring and firing decisions of firms to the point of increasing labor costs significantly. The result of paying people to be unemployed and making hiring and firing more expensive is predictable—higher unemployment that lasts longer and is less effective at controlling inflation.

In addition to discussing what we can learn from the European community about unemployment, Chapter 5 discussed the Swedish approach to unemployment and what we can learn from it. What lessons related to unemployment insurance and social welfare should the United States learn from Sweden in order to avoid the high unemployment of most of Europe and enjoy the low unemployment that Sweden had for so long?

The first lesson for the United States to learn is that if unemployment is generously subsidized with few restrictions and lengthy time limitations, more people will choose unemployment and will remain unemployed for longer periods of time. The United States can improve its unemployment insurance program without increasing direct monetary benefits and thus avoid the risk of causing higher unemployment, by improving information flows, using unemployment benefits to subsidize training costs, and allowing those unemployed who lack basic skills the option of getting those skills. Information flows could be improved by establishing, as part of the unemployment insurance program, a national database of job openings that state job service agencies could access in helping the unemployed quickly find suitable jobs. Training or retraining of unemployed workers could be improved by giving state job service agencies the option of using unemployment insurance funds to subsidize part of the wages of unemployed workers that employers agree to hire and train. Some unemployed workers lack the basic skills to be retrained. These workers should have the option of enrolling in programs that teach those basic skills and have part or all of the tuition costs paid for.

A related lesson for the United States to learn is that other social welfare payments besides unemployment insurance, if they are meant for working-age people, can affect work incentives and thus unemployment. This brings us into the realm of welfare reform. A few comments are appropriate.

As pointed out in Chapter 5, our current system of welfare is not working, and welfare reform is needed. Both conservatives and liberals agree with this, and a rough consensus has been reached on what should be done. At the most basic level, the consensus is that a welfare system that spends money better can be built. The primary features of this system would include making the clearest possible distinction between people who can and cannot fend for themselves; developing governmental policies that assure a decent standard of living for those who cannot fend for themselves; and developing policies that provide assistance and stern incentives for those who can fend for themselves to get them into the workforce and stable families and keep them there.[3]

Robert Reischauer has further delineated the centers of the emerging welfare reform consensus. He states that the consensus centers on five broad themes: responsibility, work, family, education, and state discretion.[4] Chapter 5 asked which parts of the welfare reform consensus can be recommended strictly on the basis of trying to improve the U.S. unemployment rate. In general, any reform that strengthens work incentives and/or removes incentives to simply pick up a benefit check and do nothing would reduce reservation wages and help improve the unemployment situation. Virtually all of the parts of the welfare reform consensus identified by Reischauer have the potential to help reduce the U.S. unemployment rate. Let us therefore enact welfare reform that incorporates this consensus.

One final comment before leaving the subject of unemployment insurance and social welfare payments. The recent theoretical and empirical work of Edmund Phelps adds weight to the recommendations made in this book concerning reformation of the unemployment insurance and social welfare programs. Phelps has not only analyzed the impact of social welfare programs on unemployment but has also looked at the effect of public debt and payroll taxes on unemployment. Increases in social welfare programs worldwide have contributed to an increase in public debt and thus to high real interest rates, and increases in our social welfare programs have been financed largely through increased payroll taxes. Phelps's theoretical and empirical work shows that both of these may have contributed to an increase in the U.S. unemployment rate.[5]

THE UNION WAGE PREMIUM

Labor unions can increase the NAIRU by causing business's most important cost, the cost of labor, to increase at a rate faster than justified by productivity increases. In Chapter 6, we examined the facts and reviewed the literature on three subjects to see if labor unions have contributed to an increase in the NAIRU. First, we examined the union wage premium and concluded that it increased significantly, probably doubling, in the 1970s, and it did not decline in the 1980s. We then looked at changes in union density. Union membership as a proportion of non-farm employment stood at about 32 percent in 1960. By 1992, it had declined to about 16 percent. Much of that decline came in the 1980s. During the 1970s, when the union wage premium was increasing, union density declined by only three percentage points, from about 27 percent to about 24 percent. This decline in union density was not nearly large enough to offset the large increase in the union wage premium. In other words, in spite of the decline in union density, the total amount of money being paid out as a union wage premium increased in the 1970s.

The union effect on business costs and thus on the NAIRU operates not only through union members' wages but also through how nonunion wages are affected by unionization. Thus, how important the union wage premium is in explaining the increase in the U.S. NAIRU rate depends, at least partly, on how big the union wage spillover was in the 1970s. We have not been able to come up with a firm number on the percentage of nonunion workers who were influenced by union wages in the 1970s, but we do have reason to believe that the percentage was not small. A good guess is that the union sphere of influence probably extended to at least 35-40 percent of all workers. This includes the 25 percent who were actually union members and another 10 to 15 percent who were subject to a union spillover effect.

The union wage premium and union sphere of influence numbers together suggest that unions may have contributed significantly to the 1970s increase in the NAIRU. Union density has declined significantly since the 1970s. Union wage and fringe benefit spillover has probably also declined. But the union wage premium remains at high levels in spite of the decline in union density and spillover. Unions, under current labor law, still enjoy most of the protections and special privileges derived from the fears and desires of politicians and workers in the early part of the twentieth century. This book recommends that these special privileges be taken away and that unions be allowed to compete with other forms of employee representation. This would effectively take away the monopoly power that has allowed unions in the past and could allow them in the future, to achieve a high wage premium. Labor unions do not need to be outlawed, but the NLRA and other labor laws that give unions special privileges do need to be overhauled.

At the end of Chapter 6, we briefly discussed another law that has the effect of raising target real wages and total costs in the economy—the Davis-Bacon Act. We noted that most estimates of the effects of Davis-Bacon show that it raises construction costs on projects under its jurisdiction by around 20-25 percent. Twenty percent of all construction in the United States falls under the jurisdiction of the Davis-Bacon Act. The act has few benefits and should be repealed; such was even recommended by the Government Accounting Office in 1979.

LABOR LAW, COOPERATION AND PRODUCTIVITY

In Chapter 7, a couple of aspects of the NLRA were discussed in some detail, namely, those aspects that deal with labor-management cooperation. As part of the major overhaul previously suggested, let us repeal section 8(a)(2) of the act. A brief review of the arguments in Chapter 7 that lead to this conclusion follows.

Chapter 7 began with the argument that unions may affect unemployment not only by increasing costs through the union wage premium but also by reducing productivity. The chapter then reviewed the literature on the union productivity effect and found it inconclusive. It then looked at the possibly negative impact that the National Labor Relations Act (NLRA) has on productivity through its basis on an adversarial model of industrial relations. The chapter concluded that the NLRA is, indeed, based on an adversarial model of industrial relations that is incompatible with labor-management cooperation. A review of the judicial history of the act reveals that virtually all labor-management committees, quality circles, and so on can be defined as labor organizations under Section 2(5) of the act, and virtually all labor-management committees, quality circles, and so on can be found to be in violation of Section 8(a)(2) of the act, which prohibits company unions.

Does the type of cooperation prohibited by the NLRA have a positive impact on productivity? Chapter 7's survey of the literature indicates that cooperation, when combined with an effective reward-sharing system, does have a significant positive impact on productivity. Cooperation should be encouraged, not discouraged, as a way to reduce the U.S. unemployment rate. Hence, at the very least, Section 8(a)(2) of the NLRA should be repealed.

Let us also enact some mild encouragement of a gain-sharing type of labor-management cooperation that includes employee participation in both decision making and economic rewards. This could perhaps be done by giving those companies that institute bona fide gain-sharing systems a tax break.

PRODUCTIVITY

Chapter 7 was not the only chapter to focus on productivity. In Chapter 8, we discussed how improvements in productivity can reduce the U.S. unemployment rate. Let us conclude with a discussion of this very important issue, which we dealt with so briefly in Chapter 8.

Productivity growth provides the basis for growth of feasible real wages. It is, therefore, critical to any analysis of the unemployment rate. If productivity growth is strong, then feasible real wage growth will be strong, and increases in wages will not exert inflationary pressure and thus affect unemployment.

Chapter 8 pointed out that, beginning in the late 1960s, productivity growth definitely slowed, and so the growth in feasible real wages slowed. No consensus has yet been reached on the causes of the productivity slowdown, but for our purposes such a consensus is not necessary. As long as we can identify factors that will effectively improve productivity growth, we will have a set of tools we can use to improve feasible real wage growth and attack the high unemployment problem.

Throughout this book, policies have been discussed, the primary purpose of which may not be to improve productivity growth, but nevertheless productivity growth will be improved by their implementation. Such policies come doubly recommended. Let us review briefly these policies.

As already reviewed, Chapter 3 discussed mismatch unemployment. Mismatch and/or demographic factors not only have been linked to an increase in the unemployment rate but also have been linked by some analysts to the productivity growth slowdown. If structural change did, indeed, contribute to the productivity growth slowdown, then any policies meant to combat structural unemployment should also have a positive effect on productivity growth. One major recommendation concerning mismatch unemployment is to build a world-class education system. This is one of the most important things that we can do to improve average productivity in the United States. Better-educated and better-trained employees are more productive employees. Educational reform, including choice, thus also comes doubly recommended.

Chapter 4 concerned itself mainly with government regulations. Do government regulations, besides boosting business costs, also reduce productivity growth? At first glance, it would seem obvious that government regulations reduce productivity growth because they increase costs. In other words, they increase the number of person-hours needed to produce any given level of output. Remember that productivity is usually measured as output per person-hour. This simple explanation may not be accurate. Some analysts have argued that government regulations actually increase output, but perhaps not the type of output that shows up in productivity numbers. For instance, cleaner air or safer workplaces can, in a sense, be considered outputs. Do regulations add enough to output, whether measured or not, to justify their costs? This is another way of asking for the cost-benefit calculus of government regulations and another reason for requiring cost-benefit analyses to accompany all new regulations. We need to know if the output gains due to government regulations are worth the costs. This book's recommendations on government regulations should help to limit the negative effects that government regulations can have on productivity growth.

This book has also made some recommendations regarding social welfare. Would these recommendations perhaps also help improve productivity growth? A couple of our recommendations on reforming the unemployment insurance system dealt with the training, retraining, and basic education of unemployed workers. If the implementation of these recommendations resulted in better-educated and better-trained workers, then they would result in better U.S. productivity growth. The same can be said of our recommendations on welfare reform. If the welfare system could be reformed so as to put better-educated people into the workforce, then productivity, on average, would improve. Social welfare reform also comes doubly recommended as a tool to reduce unemployment.

What about the recommendations concerning labor unions? The first recommendation is to remove all union special privileges by repealing the NLRA. Lacking this step, let us at least repeal Section 8(a)(2) of the NLRA, which currently prohibits many types of labor-management cooperation. Either one of these policies, if implemented, would likely result in improved productivity growth. As reviewed previously, the effect of unions on productivity growth is unclear, but the effect of a good cooperative system is not. Cooperation coupled with a sharing of rewards has been shown to improve productivity. One of the main reasons to reform our labor laws is the promised rewards in the area of productivity growth and thus the promised improvement in NAIRU. The same argument applies to recommendations concerning gain-sharing systems.

In summary, virtually all of the policy recommendations made in this book to reduce the U.S. NAIRU can be doubly recommended because they have the potential to improve U.S. productivity growth.

CONCLUSION

Let us now return to the unemployed welder whose experience began our discussion in Chapter 1. How would his experience have been different with this book's recommendations in place? First, our friend would have been the product of an excellent education system. As such, he would have been quite productive and very trainable. If, for one reason or another, he was still let go, he would have had access to a nationwide database of available jobs. He probably could have found a job quite quickly without having to go through all of the pain he described.

If necessary, his state job service agency could even have offered a training subsidy to an employer who agreed to hire him, thus further speeding his return to work and helping ensure that his value to this employer or another was such that he would have few unemployment episodes in the future.

Once at work, our friend's productivity and thus value to the company may have been further enhanced through his participation in a labor-management cooperative effort. His real wages and thus his standard of living could rise faster than otherwise would have been possible as the result of not only how productive he was but also how productive his company was and the entire economy were. This enhanced productivity would have been at least partly the result of a system of government regulations that carefully and effectively weighed the costs and benefits of each regulation and refused to impose unnecessary costs on business.

A high NAIRU costs the U.S. economy too much. It can, as outlined in this book, be effectively reduced without risking an acceleration of inflation. Let us not follow the example of some European countries that have found higher and higher levels of unemployment necessary to stabilize inflation. The costs of using unemployment to control inflation are too high, and we have other tools we can employ that will enable both lower unemployment and stable inflation. Some evidence already exists that because of changes in social welfare programs, declines in labor union power, and increases in productivity, the U.S. NAIRU has begun to come down. Let us hasten its decline.

NOTES

1. David R. Henderson, "The Europeanization of the U.S. Labor Market," *The Public Interest* 113 (Fall 1993), pp. 66-81.

2. For examples see ibid.; Richard Layard, Stephen Nickell, and Richard Jackman, *Unemployment: Macroeconomic Performance and the Labour Market* (Oxford, England: Oxford University Press, 1991).

3. James S. Denton, "Introduction," in James S. Denton (ed.), *Welfare Reform: Consensus or Conflict?* (Lanham, MD: University Press of America, 1988).

4. Robert Reischauer, "The Welfare Reform Legislation: Direction for the Future," in P. Cottingham and D. Ellwood (eds.), *Welfare Policy for the 1990s* (Cambridge: Harvard University Press, 1989), pp. 10-40.

5. Edmund S. Phelps, *Structural Slumps: The Modern Equilibrium Theory of Unemployment, Interest, and Assets* (Cambridge: Harvard University Press, 1994).

BIBLIOGRAPHY

Abraham, Katharine G. "Mismatch and Labour Mobility: Some Final Remarks." In Fiorella Podoa Shioppa (ed.), *Mismatch and Labour Mobility*. New York: Cambridge University Press, 1991, pp. 453-85.

Abraham, Katharine G., and Katz, Lawrence F. "Cyclical Unemployment: Sectoral Shifts or Aggregate Disturbances?" *Journal of Political Economy* 94 (1986), pp. 507-22.

Addison, John T. "Are Unions Good for Productivity?" *Journal of Labor Research* 3 (Spring 1982), pp. 125-38.

_____. "What Do Unions Really Do?" *Journal of Labor Research* 4 (Spring 1985), pp. 127-46.

Addison, John T., and Barnett, A. H. "The Impact of Unions on Productivity." *British Journal of Industrial Relations* 20 (July 1982), pp. 145-62.

Addison, John T. and Hirsch, Barry T. "Unions Effects on Productivity, Profits, and Growth: Has the Long Run Arrived?" *Journal of Labor Economics* 7 (January 1989), pp. 72-105.

Allen, Steven. "The Effect of Unionism on Productivity in Privately and Publicly Owned Hospitals and Nursing Homes," *Journal of Labor Research* 7 (Winter 1986), pp. 59-68.

_____. "Unionized Construction Workers Are More Productive." *Quarterly Journal of Economics* 99 (May 1984), pp. 249-74.

Bemmels, Brian. "How Unions Affect Productivity in Manufacturing Plants." *Industrial and Labor Relations Review* 40 (January 1987), pp. 241-253.

Blanchard, Olivier and Diamond, Peter. "The Beveridge Curve." *Brookings Papers on Economic Activity* 1 (1989). pp. 1-60.

Boal, William M. "Unionism and Productivity in West Virginia Coal Mining." *Industrial and Labor Relations Review* 43 (April 1990), pp. 390-405.

Borsch-Supan, Axel H. "Panel Data Analysis of the Beveridge Curve: Is There a Macroeconomic Relation Between the Rate of Unemployment and the Vacancy Rate?" *Economic* 58 (August 1991), pp. 279-97.

Brazier, Nona M. "Stop Law That Hurts My Minority Business." *Wall Street Journal*, January 12, 1994, p. A10.

Brown, Charles; Hamilton, Jones; and Medoff, James. *Employers Large and Small.* Cambridge: Harvard University Press, 1990.

Brown, Charles, and Medoff, James. "Trade Unions in the Production Process." *Journal of Political Economy* 86 (June 1978), pp. 355-78.

Bruno, Michael, and Sachs, Jeffrey D. *Economics of Worldwide Stagflation.* Cambridge: Harvard University Press, 1985.

Carlson, Keith M. "How Much Lower Can the Unemployment Rate Go?" *Federal Reserve Bank of St. Louis Review* 70 (July/August 1988), pp. 44-57.

Clark, Kim B. "The Impact of Unionization on Productivity: A Case Study." *Industrial and Labor Relations Review* 33 (July 1980a), pp. 451-69.

_____. "Unionization and Productivity: Micro-Econometric Evidence." *Quarterly Journal of Economics* 95 (December 1980b), pp. 613-39.

_____. "Unionization and Firm Performance: The Impact on Profits, Growth, and Productivity." *American Economic Review* 74 (July 1984), pp. 893-919.

Clark, Shaun G. "Rethinking the Adversarial Model in Labor Relations: An Argument for Repeal of Section 8 (a)(2)." *Yale Law Journal* 96 (July 1987), pp. 2021-50.

Connerton, M.; Freeman, Richard B.; and Medoff, James L. "Productivity and Industrial Relations: The Case of U.S. Bituminous Coal." Mimeographed, Harvard University, Cambridge, MA, 1983.

Curme, Michael A., and MacPherson, David A. "Union Wage Differentials and the Effects of Industry and Local Union Density: Evidence from the 1980s." *Journal of Labor Research* 12 (Fall 1991), pp. 419-27.

Dawson, Graham. *Inflation and Unemployment: Causes, Consequences and Cures.* Brookfield, VA: Edward Elgar, 1992.

Denison, Edward F. "Explanations of Declining Productivity Growth." *Survey of Current Business*, August 1979, pp. 1-24.

Denton, James S. *Welfare Reform: Consensus or Conflict?* Lanham, MD: University Press of America, 1988.

Eatwell, John; Milgate, Murray; and Newman, Peter. *The New Palgrave: A Dictionary of Economics.* New York: Macmillan, 1987.

Epstein, Richard A. "A Common Law for Labor Relations: A Critique of the New Deal Labor Legislation." *Yale Law Journal* 92 (July 1983), pp. 1357-1408.

Even, William E., and Macpherson, David A. "The Impact of Unionism on Fringe Benefit Coverage." *Economics Letters* 36 (1991), pp. 87-91.

Fosu, Augustin Kwasi. "Unions and Fringe Benefits: Additional Evidence." *Journal of Labor Research* 5 (Summer 1984), pp. 247-54.

_____. "Nonwage Benefits as a Limited-Dependent Variable: Implications for the Impact of Unions." *Journal of Labor Research* 24 (Winter 1993), pp. 29-43.

Foulkes, Fred K. *Personnel Policies in Large Nonunion Companies.* Englewood Cliffs, NJ: Prentice-Hall, 1980.

Frantz, J. R. "The Impact of Trade Unions on Production in the Wooden

Household Furniture Industry." Senior honors thesis, Harvard University, Cambridge, MA, March 1976.

Franz, Wolfgang (ed.). *Structural Unemployment*. New York: Springer-Verlag, 1992.

Fraundorf, Martha Norby; Farrell, John P.; and Mason, Robert. "The Effect of the Davis-Bacon Act on Construction Costs in RuralAreas." *Review of Economics and Statistics* 66 (February 1984), pp.142-46.

Freeman, Richard B. "The Effect of Unionism on Fringe Benefits." *Industrial and Labor Relations Review* 34 (July 1981), pp. 489-509.

_____. "In Search of Union Wage Concessions in Standard Data Sets." *Industrial Relations* 25 (Spring 1986), pp. 131-45.

Freeman, Richard B., and Medoff, James L. *What Do Unions Do?* New York: Basic Books, 1984.

Friedman, Milton. "The Role of Monetary Policy." *American Economic Review* 58 (March 1968), pp. 1-17.

Gerston, Larry N.; Fraleigh, Cynthia, and Schwab, Robert. *The Deregulated Society*. Pacific Grove, CA: Brooks/Cole, 1988.

Gordon, Robert J. *Macroeconomics*, 4th ed. Boston: Little, Brown, 1987.

Hahn, Robert W., and Hird, John A. "The Costs and Benefits of Regulation: Review and Synthesis." *Yale Journal on Regulation* 8 (Winter 1991), pp. 233-78.

Hazilla, Michael, and Kopp, Raymond J. "Social Cost of Environmental Quality Regulations: A General Equilibrium Analysis." *Journal of Political Economy* 98 (August 1990), pp. 853-73.

Henderson, David R. "The Europeanization of the U.S. Labor Market." *The Public Interest* 113 (Fall 1993), pp. 66-81.

Hendricks, Wallace E., and Kahn, Lawrence M. *Wage Indexation in the United States: Cola or Uncola*. Cambridge, MA: Ballinger, 1985.

Hirsch, Barry T., and Addison, John T. *The Economic Analysis of Unions: New Approaches and Evidence*. Winchester, MA: Allen and Unwin, 1986.

Hirsch, Barry T., and Link, Albert N. "Unions, Productivity and Productivity Growth." *Journal of Labor Research* 5 (Winter 1984), pp. 29-37.

Hirsch, Barry T., and Neufeld, John L. "Nominal and Real Union Wage Differentials and the Effects of Industry and SMSA Density." *Journal of Human Resources* 22 (Winter 1987), pp. 138-48.

Hodge, Scott Alan. "Davis-Bacon: Racist Then, Racist Now." *Wall Street Journal*, June 25, 1990, p. A14.

Hogler, Raymond L., and Grenrer, Guillermo. *Employee Participation and Labor Law in the American Workplace*. New York: Quorum Books, 1992.

Hopkins, Thomas D. "The Costs of Federal Regulation." *Policy Analysis*. Washington, DC: National Chamber Foundation, 1992a.

_____. "Costs of Regulation: Filling the Gaps." Report prepared for the Regulatory Information Service Center, August 1992b.

International Monetary Fund. *World Economic Outlook*. Washington, DC: IMF, May 1994.

Johnson, George E. "Do We Know Enough about the Unemployment Problem To Know What, If Anything, Will Help?" In D. Lee Bawden and Felicity Skidmore (eds.), *Rethinking Employment Policy*. Washington DC: Urban Institute Press, 1989, pp. 37-57.

Johnson, George E., and Layard, Richard. "The Natural Rate of Unemployment: Explanation and Policy." In O. Ashenfelter and R. Layard (eds.), *Handbook of Labor Economics, Volume 2*. New York: Elsevier Science, 1986, Chapter 16.

Jorgenson, Dale W., and Wilcoxen, Peter J. "Environmental Regulation and U.S. Economic Growth." *Rand Journal of Economics* 21 (Summer 1990), p. 315.

Juhn, Chinhui; Murphy, Kevin M. and Topel, Robert H. "Why Has the Natural Rate of Unemployment Increased over Time?" *Brookings Papers on Economic Activity* 2 (1991), pp. 75-126.

Kates, Nick; Greiff, Barres S.; and Hagen, Duane Q. *The Psychological Impact of Job Loss*. Washington, DC: American Psychiatric Press, 1990.

Katz, Lawrence F., and Meyer, Bruce D. "The Impact of the Potential Duration of Unemployment Benefits on the Duration of Unemployment." *Journal of Public Economics* 41 (1990), pp. 46-72.

Kendrick, John. *Interindustry Differences in Productivity Growth*. Washington, DC: American Enterprise Institute, 1983.

Kendrick, John W. and Grossman, Elliot S. *Productivity: The United States' Trends and Cycles*. Baltimore: Johns Hopkins University Press, 1980.

Layard, Richard. *How to Beat Unemployment*. Oxford, England: Oxford University Press, 1986.

Layard, Richard; Nickell, Stephen; and Jackman, Richard. *Unemployment: Macroeconomic Performance and the Labour Market*. Oxford, England: Oxford University Press, 1991.

Layard, Richard, and Philpott, John. *Stopping Unemployment*. London: The Employment Institute, 1991.

Lewis, H. Gregg. *Union Relative Wage Effects: A Survey*. Chicago: University of Chicago Press, 1986.

Lilien, David M. "Sectoral Shifts and Cyclical Unemployment." *Journal of Political Economy* 90 (1982), pp. 777-93.

Link, Albert N. "Basic Research and Productivity Increase in Manufacturing: Additional Evidence." *American Economic Review* 71 (December 1981), pp. 1111-12.

Litan, Robert E., and Nordhaus, William D. *Reforming Federal Regulation*. New Haven, CT: Yale University Press, 1983.

Locke, Edwin A.; Schweiger, David M.; and Latham, Gary P. "Participation in Decision Making: When Should It Be Used?" *Organizational Dynamics* (Winter 1986), pp. 65-79.

Long, Larry. *Migration and Residential Mobility in the United States.* New York: Russell Sage Foundation, 1988.

Lovell, C. A. Knox; Sickles, Robin C. and Warren, Ronald S., Jr. "The Effect of Unionization on Labor Productivity: Some Additional Evidence." *Journal of Labor Research* 9 (Winter 1988), pp. 55-63.

MacAvoy, Paul W. *Industry Regulation and the Performance of the American Economy.* New York: Norton, 1992.

Maki, Dennis R. "The Effects of Unions and Strikes on the Rate of Growth of Total Factor Productivity in Canada." *Applied Economics* 15 (1983), pp. 29-41.

Mansfield, Edwin. "Basic Research and Productivity Increase in Manufacturing." *American Economic Review* 70 (December 1980), pp. 863-73.

Maurer, Harry. *Not Working: An Oral History of the Unemployed.* New York: Holt, Rinehart & Winston, 1979.

McCaffery, Robert M. *Managing the Employee Benefits Program.* New York: America Management Association, 1983.

Mefford, Robert N. "The Effect of Unions on Productivity in a Multinational Manufacturing Firm." *Industrial and Labor Relations Review* 40 (October 1986), pp. 105-14.

Milkovich, George T. "Gain Sharing and Profit Sharing as Strategic Considerations." In Myron J. Roomkin (ed.), *Profit Sharing and Gain Sharing.* Metuchen, NJ: IMLR Press, 1990, pp. 109-122.

Mitchell, Daniel J. B. "Wage Pressures and Labor Shortages: The 1960s and 1980s." *Brookings Papers on Economic Activity* 2 (1989), pp. 191-231.

Mitchell, Merwin W. and Stone, Joe A. "Union Effects on Productivity: Evidence from Western U.S. Sawmills." *Industrial and Labor Relations Review* 46 (October 1992), pp. 135-45.

O'Connell, John F. "The Effects of Davis-Bacon on Labor Costs and Union Wages." *Journal of Labor Research* 7 (Summer 1986), pp. 239-53.

Ottosen, Garry K. *Making American Government Work: A Proposal to Reinvigorate Federalism.* Lanham, MD: University Press of America, 1992.

Pechman, Joseph A. *Who Paid Taxes, 1966-85?* Washington, DC: Brookings Institution, 1985.

Pencavel, John J. "The Distributional and Efficiency Effects of Trade Unions in Britain." *British Journal of Industrial Relations* 15 (July 1977), pp. 137-56.

Phelps, Edmund. "Phillips Curve, Expectations of Inflation, and Optimal Unemployment over Time." *Economica,* n.s., 34 (August 1976), pp. 254-81.

_____. *Structural Slumps: The Modern Equilibrium Theory of Unemployment, Interest, and Assets.* Cambridge: Harvard University Press, 1994.

Phillips, A. William. "The Relation between Unemployment and the Rate of Change of Money Wage Rates in the United Kingdom, 1861-1957." *Economica* 25 (1958), pp. 283-99.

Podgursky, Michael. "Unions, Establishment Size, and Intra-Industry Threat

Effects." *Industrial and Labor Relations Review* 39 (January 1986), pp. 277-84.

Rees, Albert. *The Economics of Trade Unions*, 3d ed. Chicago: University of Chicago Press, 1989.

Reischauer, Robert. "The Welfare Reform Legislation: Direction for the Future." In P. Cottingham and D. Ellwood (eds.), *Welfare Policy for the 1990s*. Cambridge: Harvard University Press, 1989, pp. 10-40.

Remarks by the President at the G-7 Jobs Conference, Fox Theater, Detroit, Michigan (Washington, DC: The White House, Office of the Press Secretary, March 14, 1994).

Reynolds, Morgan O. "Understanding Political Pricing of Labor Services: The Davis-Bacon Act." *Journal of Labor Research* 3 (Summer 1982), pp. 295-309.

_____. "Trade Unions in the Production Process Reconsidered." *Journal of Political Economy* 94 (April 1986), pp. 443-47.

Rissman, Ellen R. "What Is the Natural Rate of Unemployment?" *Federal Reserve Bank of Chicago Economic Perspectives* 10 (September/October 1986), pp. 3-17.

Rubin, Murray. "Federal-State Relations in Unemployment Insurance." In W. Lee Hansen and James F. Byers (eds.), *Unemployment Insurance: The Second Half-Century*. Madison: University of Wisconsin Press, 1990.

Russell, Raymond. "Forms and Extent of Employee Participation in the Contemporary United States." *Work and Occupations* 15 (November 1988), pp. 374-95.

Soete, Luc, and Freeman, Christopher. "New Technologies, Investment and Employment Growth." In Organization for Economic Co-operation and Development, *Employment Growth and Structural Change*. Paris: OECD, 1985, pp. 52-83.

Summary Statement of Treasury Secretary Lloyd Bentsen on Behalf of the G-7 Jobs Conference, Detroit, Michigan (Washington, DC: The White House, Office of the Press Secretary, March 15, 1994).

Summers, Lawrence H. *Understanding Unemployment*. Cambridge: MIT Press, 1990.

Sveikauskas, Catherine Defina, and Sveikauskas, Leo. "Industry Characteristics and Productivity Growth." *Southern Economic Journal* 48 (January 1982), pp. 769-74.

Troy, Leo, and Sheflin, Neil. *Union Sourcebook.* West Orange, NJ: Industrial Relations Data and Information Services, 1985.

Turnbull, Peter J. "Trade Unions and Productivity: Opening the Harvard Black Boxes." *Journal of Labor Research* 12 (Spring 1991), pp. 135-50.

Vedder, Richard K., and Gallaway, Lowell E. *Out of Work: Unemployment and Government in Twentieth-Century America.* New York: Holmes & Meier, 1993.

Vernon, Charles W. III. "The Inflation Impact Statement Program: An Assessment of the First Two Years." *The American University Law Review* 26 (Summer 1977), pp. 1138-68.

Vogel, David. "The 'New' Social Regulation in Historical and Comparative Perspective." In Thomas K. McCraw (ed.), *Regulation in Perspective.* Cambridge: Harvard University Press, 1981, pp. 155-86.

Wachter, Michael L., and Carter, William H. "Norm Shifts in Union Wages: Will 1989 Be a Replay of 1969?" *Brookings Papers on Economic Activity* 2 (1989), pp. 233-64.

_____. "Evaluating the Evidence on Union Employment and Wages." *Industrial and Labor Relations Review* 44 (October 1990), pp. 34-53.

Wagner, John A., and Gooding, Richard. "Shared Influence and Organization Behavior: A Meta-Analysis of Situational Variables Expected to Moderate Participation-Outcome Relationships." *Academy of Management Journal* 30 (September 1987), pp. 524-41.

Warner, David. "Watch the States." *Nation's Business,* November 1990, pp. 15-23.

Warren, Ronald S., Jr. "The Effect of Unionization on Labor Productivity: Some Time-Series Evidence." *Journal of Labor Research* 6 (Spring 1985), pp. 199-208.

Weidenbaum, Murray L. *Business, Government, and the Public,* 4th ed. Englewood Cliffs, NJ: Prentice-Hall, 1990.

Weidenbaum, Murray L., and DeFina, Robert. *The Cost of Federal Regulation of Economic Activity.* Washington, DC: American Enterprise Institute, May 1978.

Weiner, Stuart E. "The Natural Rate of Unemployment: Concepts and Issues." *Federal Reserve Bank of Kansas City Economic Review* 71 (January 1986), pp. 11-24.

_____. "New Estimates of the Natural Rate of Unemployment." *Federal Reserve Bank of Kansas City Economic Review* 78 (Fourth Quarter 1993), pp. 53-69.

Williams, Bruce A. "Bounding Behavior: Economic Regulation in the American States." In Virginia Gray, Herbert Jacob, and Kenneth N. Vines (eds.), *Politics in the American States: A Comparative Analysis,* 4th ed. Boston: Little, Brown, 1983, pp. 329-372.

INDEX

About the Authors

GARRY K. OTTOSEN is senior research analyst of Crossroads Research Institute in Salt Lake City.

DOUGLAS N. THOMPSON is president of Crossroads Research Institute in Salt Lake City.

ISBN 0-275-95360-2

HARDCOVER BAR CODE